The Psychology
of Stock Market
Timing

Every man who knows how to read has it in his power to magnify himself, to multiply the ways in which he exists, to make his life full, significant and interesting.
—ALDOUS HUXLEY

Peter Wyckoff

The Psychology
of Stock Market
Timing

► *Prentice-Hall, Inc.*

ENGLEWOOD CLIFFS, N. J.

© 1963 BY
PETER WYCKOFF

LIBRARY OF CONGRESS
CATALOG CARD NUMBER: 63-21061

PRINTED IN THE UNITED STATES OF AMERICA
73658—B&P

Foreword

THE stock market behavior of man is just as deserving of study as the eating, drinking and sex habits of animals—the kind of studies so popular in many of our psychological laboratories. The ticker tape of stock market transactions is as good a scientific record of human behavior as the income statement and balance sheet of a corporation's health.

The way a man performs when buying or selling stocks provides very definite clues to his character. Moreover, the mistakes an average person has made in the past are a guide to the dangers that beset him in future. Again such a study is important, because more than 18,000,000 persons have a stake in today's market.

Watching his stocks move up or down is an essential part of man's daily behavior. For some people the market takes the place of the bull fights of Spain, the gladiatorial combats of ancient Rome, the jousts of Merrie England. We have no principal national pastime. One group is interested in baseball, another prefers football, the wealthy like polo and yachting; but not until after World War II has such a widespread interest been evidenced toward securities.

The market has had occasional setbacks, to be sure, and others will inevitably occur. Yet most Americans would rather speculate than eat. No one enjoys much leisure. Everybody is working at his or her job most of the day. Nine-tenths of the stuff we do is routine. Even card playing has gone out among men— how long is it since you saw a really good poker game? We all get bored. Speculation is about the only thing that offers the same kind of thrills as big-game hunting, and a man can operate in the market right from his own desk. Call up your broker in the morning, place an order without moving from your seat, and the great adventure is on.

Between the covers of this book are some suggestions and ideas to help you to make money. Certainly, they should help you to *save* money.

Acknowledgments

GREAT indebtedness is due to Mrs. Marcelle Kelly and the Riggs National Bank of Washington, D.C., for their cooperation in furthering the publication of this book. Also, to *Forbes Magazine* and *The Analyst's Journal* for permission to reprint certain material; to M. C. Horsey & Co. for the use of all charts; and to *Challenge: The Magazine of Economic Affairs* for permitting their May, 1962, issue to be reproduced.

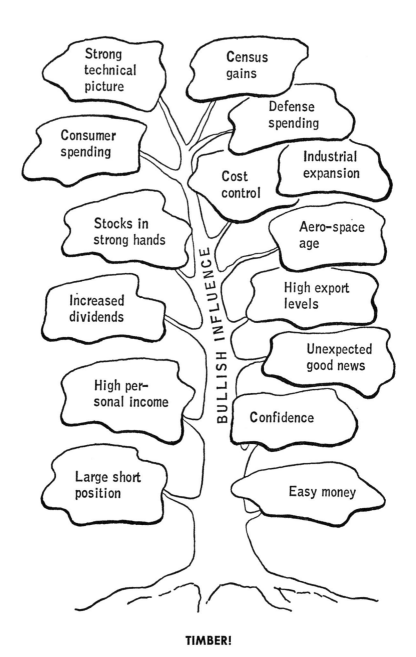

TIMBER!

Although *Wall Street is actually a one-way thoroughfare, running from West to East between a graveyard and a river, the traffic in stocks can move always in either direction—up, or down. To illustrate this fact,*

TIMBER!

the Street's symbolic "buttonwood" has been split two-for-one: to the left above are a few of the bullish factors which can influence the market's action; to the right are some of the bearish ones.

Contents

3 ▶ The Dilettante's Dilemma (Continued)

4 ▶ Touring the Market by Cycle 54

5 ▶ It Was Ever Thus 66

Section II • The Malady

6 ▶ The Trader's Trilogy 81

7 ▶ The Insiders 90

8 ▶ Blondes and Bonds 111

9 ▶ The Mood of the Bear 122

Section III • The Remedy

The Symptoms

Chapter 1

Topsy-Turvy Land, U.S.A.

FOR more than 25 years I have been in the stock market. I have feasted on bear steak and been gored by the bulls. It has been an extraordinary adventure, for I have had the opportunity to study at firsthand the quirks and foibles of human nature in the greatest human laboratory on earth—the stock market. It was like going to college on a liberal scholarship with an occasional bonus for encouragement. Whenever the market has given me back more than I put into it, I think it was because, having an insatiable curiosity about what human beings are likely to do, I have studied the market, not just from a statistical and technical standpoint, but primarily in terms of crowd behavior. After all, as Bernard Baruch said, "The stock market is people."

In the following pages I shall describe some of the mental hazards that make many people lose. I also hope to show how it should be possible to take a profit from Wall Street. For the benefit of impatient readers, there is no harm in saying right now that I believe one way to win sometimes is to do the opposite from what nearly everybody else is doing. In other words, one must be contrary occasionally, but not stubborn.

Yet I know, simple as this formula seems, few will ever follow it. Indeed, if many followed it, then it wouldn't work. If everybody tried to buy when prices are low, then bargains would never exist. A few find bargains only because the majority never recognizes bargains. The crowd generally loses, because the crowd is generally wrong. It is wrong because it behaves normally. Every natural human impulse seems to be a foe to success in stocks, and that is why success is so difficult. If you think it is easy to do the opposite of what seems to be the sensible thing that everybody else is doing, just try it. At every step one is tempted to do that which seems logical, but which nevertheless may be unwise. But more of this later.

If a successful trader, or speculator, happened to look back today on his first venture in the stock market, he might properly wonder how such a greenhorn ever dared step in at all. Certainly he would be right in saying: "What a lot I didn't know." He probably never suspected then that good news about a stock is likely to lower its price; or that bad news may force prices upward. He had not yet discovered the definite reasons why men dabbling loosely in stocks are far more likely to lose than to win. To him, the important part played by vanity in stock losses was still a sealed book. Little did he suppose that the danger of losing is greatest on Monday; that the influence of seasonal factors on the market is sometimes important. Neither did he understand why men are so inclined to sell their good securities and keep the poor ones. If he noticed that stock prices often reached their lows for the day around one o'clock in the afternoon, he undoubtedly assumed it was coincidence.

Our imaginary trader learned eventually that men win, or

lose, not so much because of economic or technical market conditions as because of human psychology. Various mental traits we all have are natural barriers to success. "Why, when I had a profit on certain stocks, didn't I sell them?" he asked himself many times. "Why did I stand by and see my profit reduced as prices drifted lower, without ever offering to sell?"

▶ *Thanksgiving Menu*

His behavior may remind you of the old man with the trap, who liked to go out into the fields to catch turkeys. The trap was a crude contrivance, consisting of a big box with a door hinged at the top. The door was kept open by a prop to which was tied a piece of string, leading back a hundred feet or more to the operator. A thin trail of corn scattered along a path lured turkeys to the box. Once inside they found an even more plentiful supply of corn. When enough turkeys had wandered inside the box, the old man would jerk away the prop and let the door fall shut. Having once slammed the door, he couldn't open it again without going up to the box, and this would scare away any turkeys lurking outside. The time to pull away the prop was when as many turkeys were inside as one could reasonably expect.

One day the old man saw a dozen turkeys in the box. Then one sauntered out, leaving eleven.

"Doggone, I wish I had pulled the string when all twelve were in there," he muttered. "I'll wait a minute and maybe the other one will go back."

But while he waited for the twelfth turkey to return, two more walked out on him.

"I should have been satisfied with eleven," the trapper told himself. "Just as soon as I get one more back I'll pull the string."

But three more walked out. Still the man waited. Having once had twelve turkeys, he disliked going home with less than eight. He couldn't give up the idea that some of the original number would return. When finally only one turkey was left in the trap, he said:

"I'll wait until he walks out, or another goes in, and then I'll quit."

The solitary turkey went to join the others and the man returned empty-handed.

The analogy to the stock market is close. When you have seen a stock go to 80 a share, you are reluctant to sell it at 78. By the time it has sunk to 75, you would gladly have taken 77. When you finally let it go at 70, you wonder what ever induced you to wait so long.

► **The Insidious Tip**

Nearly everybody is exposed to tips on the market, but the overwhelming majority of such predictions never come true. If you wonder about this and want to test it, just get a notebook and write down all the stock tips that you hear presumably intelligent people discussing. If a friend says to buy Moosepasture Oil for a quick move, jot down the suggestion in your little book. Perhaps not until several months later, when you look over the notes thus collected to see how the advance information tallied with what actually happened, will you believe that most of what one hears about stocks is false. Even after disregarding information from irresponsible people, or those who seemed unlikely to know what they were talking about, the chances are that if you had bought 10 shares of each stock that you were advised to buy, you would have been a loser.

After you have discovered that too many of the stocks most people expect to go up invariably go down, you may want to study the market more thoroughly to find out why. Is it because people are more inclined to buy poor stocks, or because they merely buy good stocks at the wrong time? The answer is that it is good stocks bought at the wrong time more often than poor stocks. Indeed, it is almost as easy to lose money on good stocks as it is on poor ones.

A person who seriously studies market trends, business cycles, industrial conditions, reactions and recoveries will discover that it is of practically no value to know that a stock is cheap, unless one also knows whether it is cheap *on the way up, or the way down.* As the late Colonel Leonard P. Ayres expressed it: "The man who buys a stock solely because of its seemingly bargain price, is like a farmer with a thermometer but no almanac, who thinks that a hot day in August must be the time to plant spring crops."

Stocks are actually a little like the weather. If you are experiencing the hottest day in several years, you may cheer up over the thought that it will surely be cooler tomorrow. Likewise, when stocks are unusually high, they are almost certain to react.

▶ Stocks on the Rocks

Before the Big Crash of October, 1929, the public had ample warning that the big fellows were selling and the little fellows buying. Week after week, published reports of the Federal Reserve Banks indicated that brokers' loans were going up, even though average stock prices were declining. In other words, the growth in loans could not be explained by greater value of stocks, for the price trend was downward. The figures could only indicate that the number of margin accounts—stocks held by brokers for customers with loans against them—were increasing, while wiser folk, able to hold their stocks outright, were selling. The only reason they could be selling was because, from their superior vantage point, they foresaw a decline and expected to repurchase stocks at lower levels. Nobody could have asked for a better hint to step out of the market. The danger signal was adequate and unmistakable. But how many heeded it?

Surely this gigantic Halloween festival, plus the September-October drop of 1937, the August-September setback in 1946, and the late tape liquidation in the spring of 1962, provide overwhelming proof that most people are generally wrong in the stock market. Otherwise, the majority would not have placed themselves in a position where they would be anxious, or compelled to dump stocks at scared-price levels. No great feat of reasoning was needed to arrive at the conclusion that these people were probably wrong or imprudent, even before the declines occurred.*

Wise men—wise, that is, as far as the market is concerned—are usually selling their stocks at the very time when the general public is most eager to buy. Indeed, the readiness of the public to buy is what gives the resourceful ones an opportunity to sell.

When the first warning break comes at the peak of a long bull uptrend, the public invariably considers this an ideal opportunity for bargain hunting and uses further available buying reserves to acquire more stocks. Naturally, this adds to the burden of protecting their holdings and increases their susceptibility to fright; and with money suddenly becoming more scarce and pessimism spreading everywhere, the volume and speed of sales pick up, until the market finally touches bottom and a period of dullness and stagnation sets in.

▶ Bargains Galore

Bargains that you never would believe in if you didn't see them are now suddenly available all through the list. But how many, except for the select few who anticipated the downtrend and now have money locked safely away, are courageous enough to buy even at these incredibly low levels? The badly frightened majority is no longer interested in bargains even if it had any money left, because it reasons: Stocks are in a violent downtrend,

---

* Even that part of the majority which had not been caught in the big market upsets of the past, and so still had money put away, did not really begin to buy until after they had seen stocks rebound substantially from their lows. Hosts of persons who had previously sold out near the bottom, decided simultaneously that the trend had changed and rushed to buy back the identical stocks—10, 20, or even 30 points higher up.

On April 1, 1963, for example, although the Dow-Jones Industrials had recovered more than 165 points from their bear market low, commission brokers complained of the continued apathy of the investing public. "Some analysts," said the *Wall Street Journal*, "fear that the public will come back into the market only when it gets too high. Brokers report that their buying orders at prices under the market are three to ten times as large as orders on their books to sell at higher than present prices. In one instance a firm has on its books orders to buy some 200,000 shares of various stocks if the prices decline, while orders to sell if prices rise total only around 13,000 shares."

therefore, they'll go still lower tomorrow! Whatever *is* will always continue.

After making, and keeping, a big fortune in Wall Street, a famous speculator was overheard to say: "I have done only what other people wanted me to. When they were determined to sell their stocks in a falling market at whatever prices they could get and clamored for buyers, I accommodated them by buying. When they were equally anxious to buy stocks at high prices, I agreeably permitted them to buy mine."

▶ Simulated Trading

Some cautious beginners, who plan to operate in the stock market, wisely do so on a make-believe basis at first, until they feel well enough equipped to test their purse and personality on the real thing. They start by making imaginary transactions and recording them in a note book. When their information about a certain stock and market conditions warrant, they buy; then if the stock advances to a level where the price seems high enough, they sell. They also make a point of selling if the stock suddenly turns sour and seems destined to go down.

Since they have no mental handicap of fear and no danger of exhausting their capital in such paper transactions, they have a distinct psychological advantage over the fellow who uses real money. It is one thing to be able to hit a target smack in the bull's-eye, but quite another thing to do so if several men are shooting at you. Most everyone learns in due course that a person who is involved with stocks at all is himself a target—always under fire. This applies especially to market pessimists, or bears, who favor the short side of stocks. As many of them discover too late: "Steeples are taller than cellars are deep."

▶ The Outsiders

It has been said with some accuracy that every so-called non-professional who operates in the stock market is an authority on at least two subjects: his principal business, or profession, and (for anyone who will listen) the science of investment and speculation.

No matter who he is, or how competent he may be in his own field, he invariably has rock-bound theories about the markets, and how they may be harnessed to satisfy his purposes and obliged to yield a golden harvest of profit.

Two or three round-trip trades lend him an air of authority when speaking about the market (no other field of economic endeavor seems so quickly to confer a certificate of mastership). A few more transactions, depending upon their degree of success, seem to qualify him to advise friends and pass along information from the "inside" as to how such and such a stock will perform, or to forecast corporate earnings and dividends.

In no other branch of economic activity do badly informed amateurs so overwhelmingly outnumber trained specialists as in the securities business. In the majority of instances the amateur could get more information than he actually takes the time and trouble to obtain before he commits himself to a stock. But it is also a fact that the task of obtaining *all* the data which a painstaking person might require necessitates more study and work, and above all patience, than the average individual is usually prepared to expend. Indeed, some persons either have no investment objective at all (except for liking stocks that will go up), or they have an impossibly diversified one: "I want quality growth stocks paying 6 per cent, with strong safety features and an outstanding appreciation potential."

Even after buying a steady dividend payer for long-term investment purposes, instead of waiting for the newspaper to report the fluctuations, they call up their broker two or three times daily. If they incur an expensive loss, they realize that they might now be obliged to forget about the market altogether; but if they make a profit, they become too sure of themselves and quit trying to learn. Remember that anyone in the market is at least getting a valuable education at Wall Street's expense!

After a year or two of observing the securities markets and making several trades, any intelligent person should discover a long list of blunders that nearly everyone makes—errors that can nearly always be considered normal crowd behavior. We all have made them and still make our full share. The following chapters will try to cover some of the mistakes most commonly made, just by way of pointing out what the average person is most likely to do.

► Running in Circles

Summing it up in advance, a brief outline of the average man's behavior in a strongly advancing market is something like this: he buys timidly at first, very little, if any, at low prices, but gains confidence as advance continues and buys more. He takes small profits but, noting that stocks still advance, he is sorry he sold and buys the same stocks back higher up. This time he determines to get more profit, but waits too long to sell and sees prices decline. Then he mistakenly sees each lower price as a bargain and buys more. Later, when the financial pages of news-

```
                    Prices
          then              fall
        up here            a point
        stocks             or two
         back               in a
       and buys            day or
       bullish            two and
       turns               every
       trader              trader
       and every           turns
        or two            bearish
       in a day           on the
        or two            market
         a point           and
         they rise       sells
           then      stocks
              down here
```

papers are full of discouragement and stocks have touched bottom, he gets scared and sells his entire holdings for less than the lowest price he paid. Taking into account brokerage commissions in and out, and federal and state taxes, small wonder that one may lose even when the basic market trend is up.

As R. W. McNeel points out in *Beating the Stock Market,* a whirlwind trader's experience in the market may be something like the circular pattern shown on page 27.

TOPICS:

- Human nature is your greatest enemy to stock market success.

- Few people find bargains in the market, because the majority never recognizes bargains.

- The crowd generally loses, because crowd psychology is usually wrong.

- The contrariness of the market is shown by the way it tends to advance on bad news and decline on good news.

- The old man and the turkeys.

- It is almost as easy to lose money on good stocks as it is on bad stocks.

- How the whirlwind trader operates.

RULES:

1. The overwhelming majority of tips never come true.

2. You should study the stock market, not just from a statistical and technical standpoint but primarily in terms of crowd behavior.

3. Make only imaginary trades in the market at first and keep a record of them, plus all the tips you hear and the outcome, in a notebook.

4. Before committing yourself in a stock, get as much information about the company as you possibly can.

5. Never try to "shoot the moon."

Chapter 2

Where
Being Illogical
Is Wisdom

ONE of the first things a person may discover about the stock market is that seemingly logical behavior is almost certain to be wrong behavior.

Indeed, one of the most charming features of the market is that one may prosper there by being illogical. Or at any rate, one's chances for success are greatly enhanced by doing what *seems* to be illogical. To follow mere obvious, surface logic is very often fatal.

Of course, some pessimists hold that the stock market itself is illogical; that any form of speculation not only is dangerous, but also downright wicked. Profits derived thereby represent ill-gotten gains (say they), because they were not won by the traditional sweat of one's brow.

It is nonetheless true that even the most conservative and successful manufacturer is also a speculator. He has to be. If he doesn't buy raw materials when they are cheap, when the market is advantageous, at least part of the time, he will finally go bankrupt. No matter how clever a salesman or advertiser a man may be, he cannot withstand the odds against him if he buys always at top prices and sells the finished product in a falling market.

Even buying a home is speculative. Certainly no one would care to own a house on land that might decline in value. And who can dispute the fact that marriage is the greatest speculative venture of them all?

▶ Speculation Is No Snap

Perhaps the very difficulty of speculation is why some people are against it. Many men who enter business fail eventually, because they are unable to become successful buyers and sellers. Likewise, men who trade frequently in and out of volatile, speculative stocks—the reach-for-it-and-grab type of speculators—will lose most of the money they risk. Naturally, the people who fail in such an enterprise are not inclined to speak too highly of it. But neither do those who have been unable to master golf mention the game in terms of the highest praise. The fact remains that an occasional man speculates in the stock market as his sole means of livelihood and continues to do so year after year. He is generally intelligent and honest, and, because he knows he is speculating, will always limit his risks. He may not become wealthy; if he did he would have no need to speculate. Yet neither does he become bankrupt; if he did he couldn't speculate.

▶ Angel or Devil?

An example of how the market frequently discourages logical thinking is the tendency of a stock to decline on good news and advance on bad news. If you own the stock of a certain company and learn that the dividend will be increased you may expect to be pleased. You might even say to yourself: "Now that dear old stock will climb. I'll pick up a dandy profit in the next few days."

But instead of advancing angelically, the stock more often will decline wickedly on the news. This is because the market has already discounted the expected event. Wall Street is filled with surprises.

Many professional market operators have reasoned that there is no use holding the stock any longer, because the bullish news they hoped for, and which the stock itself anticipated by gradually increasing in value, has now happened. Since there are suddenly more sellers than buyers, the first move of the stock when the news becomes public is downward—such as occurred on January 10, 1962 when Ford Motor Co. opened 1½ points lower and then closed off four points on the day after a 2-for-1 split and an increase in the dividend was announced. On the other hand, when prices appreciate on bad news, it is because influential people think to themselves: "The worst has now happened. The stock may not be so cheap again. Let's buy it."

▶ Buying High and Selling Low

The most logical thing the average individual can do, indeed, wnat he is most likely to do, is to buy when prices are high and sell when they are low, thus suffering a loss. Unwise as this is, it is nevertheless logical, because when stock prices are at, or near, their peak the majority of news and information one hears, or reads, is favorable, suggesting that soon they will be higher still. But when prices are at their lowest ebb, all that one learns from newspapers, or from conversation with knowing friends, is discouraging. To a mind that works logically, it appears obvious that the worst is still to come; that the end of the downward swing is not yet in sight. No wonder that most people tend to buy near the top and sell near the bottom.

▶ Why You Missed the Boat

Under such circumstances, not only will you buy toward the top, but you are likely to buy at the *exact* top. Well, why not? Never does the market for a stock appear so bullish as on the day it reaches a record high. It was favorable news that made it go there, and it was the same alluring tidings that prompted others to buy. Every evening you discover that if you had only bought certain issues when the market opened that day and sold them at the close at 3:30 P.M., you would have had a nice profit. Naturally, your hindsight vision is 20/20, and, since you also have a logical mind, you say to yourself: "The thing to do is buy these stocks tomorrow and catch the rise from now on."

Anybody knows that when a thing has happened several times over, the presumption is in favor of its continuing to happen in the same way. (Stage magicians recognize this trait of human nature and capitalize upon it. You have seen a magician toss balls into the air one after another, until finally the last ball he throws mysteriously disappears—only, he didn't throw the last ball, but just made the motion of throwing it. Most of the audience is positive he really threw it—because that was what he *had been* doing.) It is this disposition to expect a stock to continue in the same direction that it has been going, which leads people to buy at top levels after several days' rise, or to sell near the bottom after several days of decline. Because you have thus arrived at a logical conclusion, on the very day that you decide to buy, the stock goes not up, but down.

▶ **Mental Strain Is Universal**

We are inclined to think it a strange coincidence that immediately after we bought, our stock ceased to go up, and that it stopped going down after we sold. This is because we can stand just so much strain. The same influence that makes a person finally yield to buying or selling pressure compels nearly everyone else to do the same thing. The reason you are likely to buy very close to the exact top figure, or sell near the bottom, is simply because you are an average person. Naturally, when all who are inclined to buy have bought and there are no longer more buyers than sellers. the easiest direction for the stock to move is downward.

▶ Logic Can Be Dangerous

But, if you have a logical mind, you do not get excited as your stock settles lower. Looking back, you now realize that it could not have kept advancing without a normal correction. The setback, you imagine, is only temporary. Yet each day thereafter, let us say, it reacts further. After it does this for a few days, you repeat the logical reasoning you followed when it was moving up. You now decide that it will probably continue to trend lower. But the day you sell is reasonably certain to mark the end of the decline, because *you were not the only one* who was finally scared into selling. Being an average man, you were merely representative of many other people who have also sold. Since the immediate selling pressure has now been lifted, the stock suddenly stops going down.

▶ Blue Monday

Psychologists know that nearly all members of the human race are influenced somewhat by days of the week. Men do not feel the same toward the world on Monday as they do on Wednesday, or Friday, and this even affects their attitude toward buying or selling securities. That being true, wouldn't Monday be a logical day for most people to buy stocks? They have been to church the day before and received a spiritual comfort, which created in them a happy, optimistic frame of mind. Moreover, since Monday is the first day of the new business week, everybody else is starting off with high hopes. If you buy on Monday, you have your stocks all ready to participate in the advance, as the week and the market gain momentum. What then could be more natural than for most people inclined to buy stocks at all to do so on that day? However, being a bit more shrewd than the crowd, you ask yourself if it wouldn't be the cagey move to sell your stocks on Monday, when most people are buying?

Nevertheless, despite the seemingly unassailable logic of outwitting the crowd by selling your stocks on Monday, the cold fact is that Monday is the worst day of the week, in the long run, for selling and a good day for buying. In a strong bull market you are likely to find bargains on Monday. A study of the action of the Dow-Jones Industrial Stock Average over a recent three-year period showed that the 30 representative issues advanced on 65 Mondays, compared with 91 Mondays of declining action.* To be sure, the worst days of the 1929 crash were a Tuesday in October and a Wednesday in November. However, the low prices reached on both these days were a culmination of the selling that began and gathered momentum on the preceding Monday; also, the low of the 1962 market blitz was reached on a Monday—June 25.

▶ Is Sunday a Rest Day?

Men who have been to church on Sunday—and people inclined to speculate, or gamble, invariably attend church—probably heard there more gloom than good cheer. Departing from logic and looking facts in the face, one remembers that preachers, picturing the terrors of the hereafter, usually fill their listeners more with grim foreboding than elation. In other words, they try to round up sinners by fear more often than by hope. Moreover, it is on Sunday when a speculator is home from the office that his wife has a chance at him. When she sees him staring gloomily at the financial page with a what's-the-use expression on his face,

---

* When anyone asks: "How's the stock market?" reference is made generally to the state of the market in terms of the Dow-Jones Averages, which include 65 leading stocks—30 Industrials, 20 Railroads, 15 Utilities. Thus, if the market is said to be "up," or "strong," it means that the average is higher than its previous closing level. Conversely, if the market is "off," or "weak," the average is presumed to be below the previous day's close.

This connotation is obviously wrong. For, if most stocks are dormant, or trending lower, but the average of 30 stocks representing the D-J Industrials happens to be above its closing level of the day before, it should not imply that the whole market is up.

The fallacy or accuracy of the Dow-Jones Averages, or any other averages, as a yardstick of market measurement is therefore readily debatable. Too many new factors must be taken into account to enable any one set of averages to mirror exactly the entire market pattern. It is true, nonetheless, that the D-J Averages are the oldest and probably the best-known averages now in use. Thus, when any question is asked respecting the current position of the market, up or down, the answer is generally given in terms of their prevailing status.

she is apt to exclaim: "Sidney, I want you to get out of those stocks tomorrow and stop worrying about them!" Or, there is a letter from Mary and Bill at college telling him they want more money. Mother reminds him she needs new clothes, or the kitchen needs redecorating.

Sidney, on his way to the office on Monday, wonders how in the world he is going to meet all these demands.

"Sell some stocks," is the answer.

The result is that stocks tend to decline on Mondays, even though logic demands that they do nothing of the sort.

When you think the strategic time has come to sell part of your securities, the obviously logical thing to do is to dispose of those that have risen sharply in price and keep those which have not yet had an upward move. It does not take much reasoning to conclude that the ones which have advanced the most are probably perilously high, while those which stood relatively still are less likely to drop. Hence, if you sell the issues in which you have a profit and keep the others, when the tardy ones advance you will be able to show a profit on them all.

▶ **A Kennel of Market "Dogs"**

The only trouble with this approach is that, though logical, it is often wrong. The stocks which advanced in price probably did so on their own merit, because of expanding business and the bright future outlook of the corporation they represent. Subject, of course, to occasional price corrections, they are therefore the ones most likely to keep on rising. Likewise, those that stood still did so because they were already quite fully valued. Especially in a time of forced selling, such as to meet an emergency, you are naturally inclined to sell your good quality stocks and keep the poor ones. You say to yourself: "I'll sell those that already show me a good profit and hold the others until they show a profit too."

Because of your faculty for reaching logical conclusions, you have sold the stocks most capable of further price appreciation and have kept those that are most likely to continue to remain dormant, or tilt downward. In the end, you may discover that you are nursing a bunch of chronic invalids.

Logically enough, the inexperienced person with 100 shares of stock costing 15 a share thinks to himself: "Oh well, the most I can lose is $1,500, even if it goes to zero." But he would often be in a far better position if, instead of having 100 shares at 15, he had 10 shares selling at 150. Stocks priced at 15 have a tendency to decline to 10 more frequently than stocks selling at 150 drop to 100. Aside from the fact that high-priced stocks usually have more merit (or they wouldn't be high-priced), low-priced stocks are more dangerous because they are especially likely to be held by people of small means, who are easily frightened and may unload them in time of stress for what they can get.

▶ Please Pass the Dividends

Another delusion is that stocks paying good dividends are less likely to go down in a falling market than those which provide only a small return. An investor would obviously prefer to hold on to that which gives him the greatest yield. But the 1962 market disproved most of this theory; and even during the bull market of several years previous, one may have noticed that many issues which behaved best during temporary setbacks and then recovered the fastest were those which paid only small or, in many cases, no dividends. Men of large means who can afford to hold stocks on a cash basis for future growth and price enhancement, and who, in fact, like small dividends, for obvious tax reasons, are among the few who cannot be scared into selling until they are good and ready.*

---

* Most stockholders would be better off financially if they never received dividends, according to Professor James Porterfield, a Stanford University stock market expert. This is because many companies can invest retained earnings more profitably than can individual shareholders.

"An increase in the dividend," claims Mr. Porterfield, "should not be interpreted as a bullish signal. Instead, it should be considered a confession by the company that it no longer has anything better to do with its funds. A reduction in the dividend—or better yet, its complete elimination—should often be regarded as a highly favorable development." (But only if earnings remain high.)

▶ *Professional Advice*

All this seems to prove that it is nearly always fatal to rely on one's own logic; so perhaps you will conclude that the shrewd thing to do is to follow the advice of others who know more about stocks than you do. Your broker must know. He deals in stocks all the time. Stocks are his business. But while the professional advice of a broker, a banker, or even an experienced and trusted friend will be valuable in helping you decide what to do, the final decision must be up to you. Of course, your own judgment is influenced by many kinds of information, which must be weighed and interpreted. A great deal of it will probably be derived from newspapers. You observe on the first page that the market is having a boom. This news has become so important that it no longer can be confined to the financial section, but has bounded to page one. With all signs indicating higher prices, it is evidently a logical time to buy stocks. Is it though? After you have bought you begin to wonder. You learn that the stock news reached the first page, not only because the market was up sharply, but also because the accompanying trading volume was unusually large. By the time you get aboard, all the traders, who saw the market advance starting have already bought. Who then is going to bid up your stocks?

▶ *The Short Side*

If stocks show a perverse tendency to sell off again the minute you buy, why not try and outsmart the market by engaging in what is known as "selling short"? In other words, why not sell stocks you have not yet acquired in the hope that in a declining market you will be able to "cover," or buy back, the same stocks at lower prices? The difference between the original selling price and the eventual buying price, if it is lower, will represent your profit in the transaction. However, the danger of following this method is that by the time you decide to sell short, your idea is so logical that it is equally obvious to other traders and speculators. If the short side of the market seems temporarily overcrowded in certain stocks (this can be determined by the size of the short selling figures published each month), the other people who have also sold short may become nervous and eager to cover their positions. If their short covering operations happen to coincide with new purchases being made by long pull investors, who may now sense undervaluation in the same stocks, prices will appreciate sharply.

▶ In Package Form

Some individuals, who despair of picking the one stock that will turn out a winner, buy several stocks in package form, hoping that at least one will be a real prize. But, as the saying goes: "There's a lemon in every basket of fruit!" In that event an illogical thing happens. While one good stock won't help the poor ones, a bad stock may contaminate all the rest. When you show a loss on one stock, you invariably will try to offset it by holding the others—even after they have advanced about as far as can be reasonably expected. Instead of selling them at peak prices, you will tend to hold on too long and may even get rid of some at a loss. It is true, too, that a man who believes most implicitly that a certain stock will advance, say, 30 or more points, is less likely to be right than if he felt less sure about it.

▶ Take Nothing for Granted

The following bit of reasoning by a trader near the close of a period of sharp reaction further illustrates the unwisdom of too logical an approach toward the market. This trader was studying a stock that had steadily resisted the downpour of selling, and was only a point or so lower than it was before the decline started.

"Any stock that can do that must be extra good," he reasoned, "therefore, when the turn does come, in a day or so, it will be one of the first stocks to recover sharply."

He bought the stock and was right about it being good, but when the upturn finally came, that stock went down more than on any one day during the decline. What probably happened was that many people who still had profits in it suddenly decided to sell out in order to raise money for purchasing faster-moving issues.

It seems that a logically minded person can hardly trust his senses. Nearly everything one sees proves to be untrue. On the Sunday following the fatal October Tuesday of 1929, when a record 16,410,030 shares cascaded on the market, newspapers around the country carried banner headlines about the flood of buying orders that would swamp the market on Monday morning. A canvas of New York brokerage houses by newspaper reporters indicated that tired clerks would scarcely be able to handle such an influx of orders from bargain hunters. This opinion seemed to substantiate John D. Rockefeller's statement: "My son and I are buying sound common stocks." But prices slipped lower all that Monday, from the opening gong right up to the close. The newspaper stories of buying orders had notified all the wiser people, who had bought a day or two previously, that now would be a better time to sell.

▶ Outsmarting the Pack

To be too logical in one's thinking toward the stock market can be dangerous and perhaps fatal. If you are logical, you are merely doing what nearly everyone else is doing. Profits in the market depend largely on *your being smarter* than the majority of people. But you can't do that if you make the identical errors that they consistently make. This same margin seems to separate those who own their own swimming pools from those who can't even keep their heads above water.

TOPICS:

- The very difficulty of speculation may be the reason why some people are against it.

- The market seems to discourage logical thinking.
- When stocks are at or near their peak most of the news and information one hears is favorable.
- People buy at top levels after several days of rise, or sell near the bottom after several days of decline, because of their tendency to expect a stock to continue in the same direction that it has been going.
- Nearly everyone is somewhat influenced by days of the week.
- When a person decides to sell part of his securities, he logically tends to dispose of those that have advanced most sharply and keep those that have not yet moved ahead.
- Some examples of the unwisdom of a too logical approach toward the stock market.

RULES:

1. Seemingly logical behavior is almost certain to be wrong behavior in the stock market.

2. People who trade frequently in and out of volatile, speculative stocks stand to lose most of the money they risk.

3. Never does the market for a stock appear so bullish as on the day it reaches a record high.

4. Monday is the worst day of the week in the long run for selling and a good day for buying.

5. It usually is better to buy 10 shares of a stock selling at 150 than 100 shares selling at 15.

6. Dividend-paying stocks are just as vulnerable to a decline as non-dividend-paying issues.

7. Profits in the market depend largely upon *your being smarter* than the majority.

Chapter 3

The Dilettante's Dilemma

MR. WEBSTER defines "dilettante" as *one who follows an art or a branch of knowledge desultorily or superficially, or as a pastime.* As applied to the stock market, the term refers to an outsider who dabbles loosely in speculative stocks as an adjunct to his regular line of work.

During the last bull market a young bank clerk who had scraped together $2,000 arranged to open a margin account with a broker. One day he telephoned to ask about prices and said:

"I'd buy 50 shares of XYZ if I had time to bring you over a check. But I'll wait until tomorrow."

"You don't need to wait," replied the broker affably. "We know you have the money ready and you can buy the stock now if you want."

That was at 11 o'clock in the morning. Near

the close of the market that same day, he sold out at a profit of nearly $235. Mind you, he hadn't yet had time to put up a cent of the money. Soon after he paid for the stock, the broker sent him a check representing the happy difference between his buying and selling prices.

Small wonder if his regular job, with a modest weekly salary, began to look downright ridiculous. He soon felt such confidence that at the end of three months his profits along with most of the original $2,000 were all gone.

▶ Scotch Caution

More painful, but far safer in the long run, was the experience of another young man, who used Scotch caution in his first market venture. "I want to buy 30 shares of UVW if it goes down to 225," he told his broker, "but I don't want to let the market ever go far against me, so as soon as you have bought it, enter a Stop Loss Order to sell if it drops back to 220."

Barely an hour later, the broker phoned to say that he had executed *both* orders! The stock had dipped down to 219⅛ and then started back up again—and the young trading novitiate was out about $160 plus taxes and brokerage commissions. Swift and sad, but a valuable lesson. He eventually made some money.

▶ Background and Training

If you were seeking employment as a mason, carpenter, plumber, or tree surgeon, it would probably be assumed by the person solicited that you had long experience in the field, or had served enough apprenticeship to qualify for the position. If the qualifications were doubtful, you would likely be tested, or required to submit references, before you were hired. If these showed that you had little or no experience, it would be considered presumptuous that you had even applied for the job.

▶ Self-Control

Dilettante traders generally disregard the fact that the stock market requires more skill and mental qualifications than most other vocations. They seem to believe that success depends largely on luck, and knowledge plays only a minor role. Such a casual mental approach forgets that speculation demands cool judgment, self-reliance, courage, pliability and prudence. Moreover, a person must be able to keep his emotions in check, have a mania for ferreting out facts and be immune to the enchantment of another's personality.

▶ Burial by Subscription

People who believe that market movements are founded on chance alone usually reason that commitments sparked by impulse or instinct will accomplish a desired result. While this approach may succeed occasionally, anyone who becomes dedicated to such a notion and persists in following it will not only be digging his own financial grave, but also will be risking a burial by subscription.

Everything works in harmony with basic laws: medicine, physics, biology, engineering, finance—virtually anything you could name. These laws are immutable. If we overlook these laws, or consistently fail to keep pace with them, a penalty will be levied which could bring permanent ill health, a bad accident perhaps, or in the case of haphazard speculation—bankruptcy.

▶ Low-Priced and Penny Stocks

Few people understand the power of mental suggestion as it influences purchases or sales of securities. This is one reason why most market dilettantes are drawn so often to low-priced issues. The price attracts them: first, because the fact that it is already low indicates that it can't go much lower; second, because they know they won't lose much even if it does go down; third, because they can buy more of that particular issue than of some other stock selling at a higher price.*

▶ **Some Have Merit**

Many low-priced stocks eventually do make good. The natural gambling instincts of most people, plus the hope of latching onto another General Motors, or an infant IBM, or a second General Electric, or an adolescent Union Carbide, offer further inducements for buying. Indeed, volumes have been written about the jackpots hit by canny individuals who stepped into a situation on the ground floor and were whisked straight to the roof. It is only natural that we try to emulate their tactics.

▶ **It's a Sleeper**

But even if a man is fortunate in buying several hundred shares of a sleeping future blue chip at fire sale prices, this still is no guarantee that he will make a profit. He may have shown initiative and imagination in taking on a line of stock in a small and obscure company and, if prior calculations are right, his chances of winning a good profit over a period of time appear reasonably bright.

However, the moment that stock is purchased the astute foresight and correct market timing he used in buying it will oftentimes become warped by myriad conflicting rumors, misinformation, reports and statements concerning the acquisition. And the greater that individual's position is in the stock, the more susceptible will he be to making a wrong move.

* Small investors are the real owners of this country's industries. Almost three-quarters of the 1,911,000 people owning American Telephone & Telegraph stock on January 1, 1961 held less than 100 shares and only 3 per cent owned 500 shares, or more. Also, the typical common stockholder of Consolidated Edison owns 40 shares and the typical preferred holder 24 shares. About 60 per cent of Con Ed's common stock outstanding is registered in the names of individuals (men, women and joint ownership). Less than 1/20 is in the names of brokers.

▶ Falling Out of Bed

If the stock drifts downward slightly after he is loaded up, he invariably will contact all his friends and acquaintances for their view of the situation. These clustered opinions, including those from people who probably know relatively little about the background of the stock concerned, are bound to have a mental effect on the holder. Unless he can stick to his original belief that the stock has definite worth, he is likely to become so confused and worried by a mixture of bad advice, that he will consequently unload his position in fear and disgust the next time the stock dips under his original buying level. Or he will quickly dispose of it on any slight rally, thereby missing on either count a strong advance which may only just then be getting started.

▶ When Your Bucks Take Wing

Even assuming that he can disregard the opinions of others about the stock and has patience to hold on for the rise he originally estimated was bound to come, he will run the risk of failing to sell at the proper time. If the highest prices reached by the stock happen to coincide with widespread optimism regarding it, or the entire market sweeps upward in a grand manner, it is unlikely that he will be able to act contrary to the overwhelming favorable Street psychology and harvest his profit. Indeed, he may actually find it difficult not to buy more. The moral is that a person's planned buying policy must dovetail with a predetermined selling policy, regardless of what the unreliable majority of people tell him to do.

A stock exchange was once defined as "an institution which perpetuates the use of an ancient punitive machine known as stocks." Originally, stocks were occupied by the lawless and entailed great physical suffering. Today they are embraced more often by haphazard speculators whose basic financial distress may be just as great.

► Speak for Yourself, John

One of the dilettante's greatest handicaps is his inability to think independently. If he is a frequent tape watcher, the electrified atmosphere of a board room will only compound his confusion, causing him to act hastily and unwisely. Because he has an urge to be always in the market, but usually cannot make up his own mind about what to do, he will be tempted to pile into some wildcat stock on a virtual stranger's say-so.

In an earlier chapter it was suggested that one way to test the value of all rumors and stock tips that you hear is to write them down in a notebook, along with the prices prevailing at the time they were given, and compare them two or three months later with current prices.

► Listing the Pros and Cons

Another method of checking yourself and curbing over-enthusiasm about buying a stock, is to write down on half a piece of paper the reasons you think that particular stock should be bought, and on the other half list all the arguments you can muster for leaving it alone. This should be done especially when you have been told to buy a stock "immediately." There is seldom any reason for lightning action in the stock market. When in doubt about what to do, do nothing! The market is open weekdays from 10 A.M. to 3:30 P.M., and there is plenty of time to act. You should think about what you intend to do, overnight at least.

► "Big Steel"

Take the action of U.S. Steel in April, 1962. Suppose you were sitting undecided in the board room of a large brokerage firm near the close of the market on the 10th of that month. You have noticed that the steel stocks have been going down rather steadily for some time, and are selling substantially below their previous highs. Are they sold out and perhaps overdue for a strong recovery? The opinion of this brokerage firm where you make your headquarters seems to favor the possibility. Moreover, a few of the men you speak to there are even quite enthusiastic that the steel wage settlement and the virtual certainty of a rise in the price of steel will spark more inflation and boost the whole market upward and onward. But you are still undecided.

Suddenly, through the cloud of mental indecision, conflicting advice and speculative *go-go-go*, let us say you get the idea that U.S. Steel is a definite buy. The stock closed April 10 at 68 a share, up ⅜ from the day before and the next morning it wafted 2¾ points higher at the opening and edged to 70⅞, with other issues ballooning commensurately on overnight news that certain steel prices had been lifted.

But "Big Steel" never went above 70⅞! Had you bought it the previous day, when you were thinking of doing so, your greatest possible profit would have been $2.87½ a share, which you undoubtedly would not have taken. Since the stock thudded lower right after that on news of the government's counter measures against the steel companies, your loss would have been very large. Early in June it declined to the low 40's.

On the other hand, had you gone off to some quiet spot by yourself and listed the actual reasons why you should buy the stock, or leave it alone, your thoughts might have been worded something like this:

TO BUY . . . The general market must be approaching a strong buying level, after declining some 40 points since the first of the year.

A spring rally should be starting soon, and first quarter earnings will be very good compared with last year. I am crazy if I don't take advantage of this chance to make some easy money by buying stocks.

General business is very favorable and steel is a basic industry that usually does well in the spring. The yield on U.S. Steel selling at 68 is about 4.4 per cent.

Now that the strike threat is over, the automobile companies and other major steel consumers will be stepping up their orders to beat the coming price boost.

I have only a few other stocks anyway and they haven't been doing too well. The profit I expect to make on just this one issue should more than offset the loss I show on the others.

. . . OR, NOT TO BUY? The fact that most of my friends think the market is a buy suggests the need for caution. The steel stocks may be cheap right now, but are they cheap on the incline, or the decline?

Foreign competition is increasing and if prices keep going up in this country, maybe we won't be able to sell so much steel abroad. Besides, a price hike would be inflationary and the government is already committed to an anti-inflation stand.

The stock has drifted lower almost consistently since the first of the year. It may be overdue for a rally, but a glance at its technical chart pattern shows that no strong base has formed and it could just as well carry downward some more.

Therefore, in buying U.S. Steel at its current price I am betting on a recovery of 4-5 points, against a possible loss of more than that. What I am actually doing is gambling that the market will go up, and if I plan to buy I must also decide beforehand when to sell. If the stock goes down instead of up, I must determine how much I can afford to lose and enter a Stop Loss Order at some prescribed level below my purchase price.

A person who followed the latter line of thought would either have left U.S. Steel alone entirely (subsequent price action showed that this would have been best), or bought the stock around 68 and been stopped out later with only a small loss.

The plus and minus factors behind any stock can be similarly tabulated and weighed. If considered carefully and slowly, with special attention being paid to the technical price pattern of the general market, they should go a long way toward curbing needless errors.

▶ Jumping In and Out

Overenthusiasm and haste about buying stocks are the rocks on which many speculative craft have been wrecked. Almost anyone can sail a boat on a clear day with a favorable breeze; but when a squall is brewing, or danger threatens, an experienced navigator is needed to save the craft from destruction. Nothing can destroy the cool temperament of a man like unsystematic speculation. A loss incurred through greedy, immature action makes him impatient to recover it, and automatically increases the chance that it will be doubled. If he is fortunate and wins back the loss, instead of pausing to reflect upon the surprise created within himself by a result he had barely hoped for, he goes on blindly tempting fate. The vicissitudes of the market will unsettle his judgment more and more, until he finally begins to overtrade frantically in almost anything that comes along. Such a person is certainly no stranger in brokers' board rooms around the country; swarming in and out of stocks, first as little bulls, then as little bears, and finally vanishing altogether like so many flies being shooed from a platter of picnic sandwiches.

▶ How Is She Doing?

Another strange tendency of many people is to refer to the market or a specific stock in the feminine gender. Thus, SHE is strong today, or SHE is quiet. Likewise, SHE may be dull, or flat; reactionary, or buoyant; firm or drooping—depending upon the character of the price action at a particular time. The same type of person does not identify BS on the ticker as Bethlehem Steel, but talks of the stock as "Bessie." In the same manner, AH is "Alice" instead of Allis-Chalmers, TS becomes "Tessie" for Texas Pacific Coal & Oil, and "Molly" is tape language for MLY, referring to Molybdenum Corporation.

Perhaps it is because the market is sometimes fickle, stubborn, or contrary and has certain other female traits, that the world's greatest auction center is so often referred to as SHE. On the other hand, maybe people use the expression because they think SHE is liable to provide them with more of the good things of life than either HE or IT! In other words, forget that "the female of the species is deadlier than the male": just handle her gently and SHE will yield almost anything that one could immediately desire.

▶ Cadillac Complex on a Hot-Rod Pocketbook

In addition to devotees of the SHE market concept is another group, which likes to translate everything it does, or currently possesses, or may wish to acquire, into terms of so many points fluctuation in the price of a stock.

A $4,500 automobile is not just a gleaming object with upholstered seats, a heater and a radio. More importantly, it represents 15 points on 300 shares of a volatile stock. And what is that after all? One day, three days, or even a week or two of trading—anybody can do that. Similarly, a trip to Europe may be won by only three or four turns in a $50 stock. That's easy too.

To be sure, the stock may be balky and demanding from her a European vacation may cause a temporary loss, but then one doesn't *have* to visit Europe at just that moment. If the trader has a family and household expenses, there always are stocks to take care of them. Consider R.C.A., for example. The timing may be wrong in buying her and maybe the stock will zig instead of zag as hoped, but Radio is available each weekday for 5½ hours and SHE can pay the rent.

▶ Heads, or Tails?

Compared with intelligent speculators who follow the thesis, "Look after the losses and the profits will take care of themselves," the average market dilettante never sets sufficient value on the importance of avoiding a loss and thinks only of the profits. The sensible precautions he ordinarily would take in his own line of business, where a 10 per cent return is considered very good, he usually ignores in speculation, from which he expects a 100 per cent yield. He is addicted to risks and he craves excitement. His rare market successes lead to frequent market excesses. Yet he always defends his foolish actions by telling himself that a stock can move only in two directions—up or down—and therefore his chances of winning are at least fifty-fifty.

▶ *Wanted: Cast-Iron Stomach*

Good speculators are rare birds, indeed. No one raises a son to be a speculator and no college offers a degree in the noble art. Most men reason that life is short and to spend it always in an atmosphere of excitement, under circumstances which keep up a constant mental strain, is a mode of making money that involves too heavy sacrifices. The person who deliberately selects such a calling must be physically and mentally well constituted.

▶ *Epigram for Wall Street*

In some respects nerve is the most important attribute of a speculator. Without it he could not coincide his actions with his opinions. He knows that impatience must never outmaneuver judgment, so he must have abundant patience too: it enables him to wait for precisely the right instant to buy and the exact moment to sell. Of course, money is necessary but, contrary to popular belief, is the least important of all the essentials. A small amount of capital, backed by plenty of nerve and knowledge, will almost increase by itself. Otherwise, the professional speculator, and for that matter the market dilettante, can always depend on this foolproof money-making method advocated by Edgar Allan Poe in his "Epigram for Wall Street."

> I'll tell you a plan for gaining wealth,
> Better than banking, trade, or leases . . .
> Take a bank note and fold it up,
> And then you will find your money in creases!
> This wonderful plan without danger, or loss,

Keeps your cash in your hands, where nothing can trouble it;
And every time that you fold it across,
'Tis as plain as the light of the day that you double it.

TOPICS:

- Dilettantes generally disregard the fact that the stock market requires more skill and mental qualifications than most other vocations.

- Three principal reasons why people are attracted to low-priced stocks.

- Buying a stock at fire sale prices is one thing, but knowing what to do later in order to hold a profit is quite another.

- One of the dilettante's greatest psychological handicaps is his inability to think independently.

- A recommended method for curbing overenthusiasm about a stock is to write down all the reasons you can think of for buying it, plus all the reasons you can think of for leaving it alone, and then checking one against the other.

- The story of "Big Steel" in April 1962.

- A psychological quirk peculiar to many people is a tendency to refer to a specific stock, or the market, as SHE. Another is to translate, or describe, everything in terms of so many points fluctuation in the price of the stock.

- The dilettante never sets sufficient value on the importance of avoiding a loss and thinks only of the profits.

- A good speculator needs abundant patience; but, contrary to popular belief, money is least important of all the essentials.

RULES:

1. Speculation demands cool judgment, self-reliance, courage, pliability and prudence.

2. Stock market movements are not just founded on chance alone.

3. A person's planned buying policy should always dovetail closely with a predetermined selling policy.

4. When in doubt about what to do in the market, do nothing.

5. Nothing can destroy the cool temperament of a man like unsystematic speculation.

6. Look after the losses and the profits will take care of themselves.

Chapter 4

Touring
the Market
by Cycle

NATURE teaches us that there is a time for everything: a time for sowing, a time for reaping; a time for living, a time for dying. Farmers now know that the laws of nature cannot be defied, and would no more try to raise pineapples in Maine than start a maple sugar farm in a Miami suburb.

The same holds true in the stock market. When stocks are overbought after a long advance and the market cycle changes, neither the bullish opinions of all the brokers and financial services in Wall Street nor the glowing forecasts made by government officials and corporate chiefs can stem the flow of selling, any more than bearish news headlines and reports, shrunken profit margins, or even the knell of doom itself can halt the tide of buying when the time is ripe for another cyclical change.

The stock market moves in definite cycles of distribution, decline, accumulation and advance. They dovetail roughly with cycles of prosperity, recession, depression and recovery in business. It is important to be able to identify and time these cycles correctly, and to anticipate corresponding changes in public psychology as far ahead as possible. As Jay Gould used to say: "The perfect operator must know when to come in; more important, he must know when to stay out; and most important, he must know when to get out once he is in."

Imagine to yourself a stock market where "normal value" is based on the law of supply and demand and on human judgment, as closely as that will-of-the-wisp factor can be pinpointed. "Normal" represents a broad trading area within which buying and selling pressures are approximately equal, speculative excesses are few, neither bulls nor bears predominate, and the daily share turnover is about average.

▶ The First Hill

The initial phase of a rise toward normal from the base of a cycle moves slowly, with little fanfare. The insiders will be accumulating, and specialty stocks and groups provide spasmodic leadership. But there is no cohesive action, or stampede to buy. The general public is still mostly bare of stocks.

Phase two is more sprightly. The market broadens and volume picks up. Public interest increases and scattered purchases are made, but people generally are quite skeptical of the upward swing so far. They prefer to wait for one more setback on which to buy. It seldom ever comes.

▶ Pedaling to the Peak

The bull market is formally identified when phase three begins. Its usual characteristics include: sharply expanding volume, wide price fluctuations, profuse offerings of new securities, optimism in the press, dividend increases and stock splits. Public confidence zooms commensurately. Bullish traders chide the bears to "Sell 'em again and get licked again." The market bounds forward 3-4-5 days in a row. Reactions are limited; those who wait for them soon get impatient and jump in "at the market." Paper profits multiply, as do the prophets. Hope and greed predominate and the market soon reaches the fireworks stage. At this point, the average broker's life is a melee of telephone calls, wires from out-of-town, buy orders, black coffee and scrambled securities, frequent late tapes and flying fractions on the bedroom ceiling.

▶ Rain or Shine

Then one day, although business and the market still appear sound and investor sentiment is bullish, without a single disturbing cloud in the sky, some leading blue chip which has been a hallmark of the bull movement plunges straight down. A special news item may have touched off the selling, such as the lung cancer controversy that chilled the tobacco stocks in 1961, but more often it is simply because the supply of stocks now exceeds the demand. Everybody is loaded to the hilt, and more sellers than buyers have appeared overnight.

This unexpected drop is usually the first warning of a possible change in the market cycle. Never disregard it, for, just as a bolt of lightning on a summer afternoon is nature's warning of an approaching storm, so is the first abrupt selloff after a sustained rise, the market's warning burp of overindulgence in stocks. The market gives no reasons or excuses for its behavior. It never explains anything. When the moment arrives for a change of trend, bells or klaxons, it soundeth not!

▶ Flat Tires

The moment a new business or novelty item becomes so popular that those who started it make big money, the rush by others to join in the fun will cause overproduction and lower prices.

Remember the mania for Davy Crockett hats; the Hula Hoop fad; the craze for pleasure boats that created a surplus manufacturing capacity? The same situation can and does prevail in the stock market when the scramble by all to get aboard all causes overcrowded conditions.

▶ Who Is Clogging the Road?

After the market has moved into orbit, following a spectacular flight, and it seems almost doubtful that enough stocks will be left to buy . . . WATCH OUT! Somehow, somewhere, either by insiders selling, new offerings of securities, or seemingly as if more certificates were printed secretly, enough stocks will be found to oblige the crowd. The buyers who were around only yesterday mysteriously disappear and, just as the sun sets below the horizon, so will distribution in the market shift into a declining cycle with lower prices all around. *Après ça le déluge!*

▶ Coasting Downhill

A further shakeout of weak stockholders from the speculative tree accompanies the first slide downhill. Then a rally follows, retracing some ⅓ to ½ of the previous ground lost. But this soon runs into stone wall resistance. In-and-out traders, who bought near the bottom of the first reaction from the top will have profits to clinch, and the professional short sellers, who covered their positions during the first big dip, will now begin putting out new lines of short stock. The decline still has further to run.

▶ Braking the Breaks

Heavy liquidation marks the second downward phase. Certain issues that resisted the initial drop begin to get hit with belated selling. Rallies are scarce. Consumer buying slackens. The business news turns discouraging. Reassuring comments from government leaders fall flat as stocks themselves. "Stand on your heads and watch 'em go up!" becomes a rallying cry of the bears.

The third and final plunge is marked by panic conditions. Confidence is at zero. Dividends are reduced or entirely omitted. Red ink figures are everywhere. Many of the same people who were the staunchest bulls at the peak of the cycle now advocate selling. A "graveyard market" condition develops, where those who are in can't get out and those who are out don't want to get in. The general sentiment finally becomes so blue that scarcely anyone would buy a stock, even if the certificate were signed by an angel of Heaven.

▶ The Turning Point

This is the time to start picking up discarded values that now are strewn everywhere throughout the list. Several months may be required before prices finally stabilize and accumulation for the long haul back upward begins. But the market will recover eventually and, as conditions improve and industry climbs to its feet, the tide of profits begins to turn; rippling back into channels where stocks have lain high and dry and neglected, it floats them into prominence again. Just as when there is no use for the tractor the farmer is idle, so when great industries are inactive, floating capital lies idle and is cheap. At such a time the investor with clear foresight and ability is in position to profit without much risk. But if he waits until every phase of uncertainty is removed and doubt is lifted, he will keep on waiting . . . waiting.

UPWARD MARKET CYCLE

	Extreme Lowest	— 0 —	Extreme Lowest.
Phase One	Gradual Improvement	— 20 —	Insiders accumulating stocks. Public is skeptical.
	General Improvement	— 35 —	Business and earnings improve. Public begins to buy.
Phase Two	*Normal Value*	— 50 —	*Normal Value.*
	Aggressive Advance	— 85 —	Corporate news is good. Money is plentiful. Public rushes in.

UPWARD MARKET CYCLE

Phase *Three* {	Boom Dullness-Stagnation	— 95 —	Public still buying. Heavy volume. All reactions are temporary. Extra dividends. Stock splits. "Cats and dogs" prominent on tape. Buying interest rotates, Insiders start to sell.
	Extreme Highest	—100—	Extreme Highest.

DOWNWARD MARKET CYCLE

	Extreme Highest	—100—	Extreme Highest.
Phase *One*	Reaction—Scattered Weakness	— 95 —	Much bullish talk. Dividend increases. More insider selling.
	General Selling	— 85 —	More bullish talk. Public starts to "average down." Insiders still selling.
Phase *Two* {	*Normal Value*	— 50 —	*Normal Value.*
	Heavy Liquidation	— 35 —	Weak holders sell out. Rallies are limited.
Phase *Three* {	Apathy	— 20 —	Market is bumping bottom. Dividends passed, or omitted. Press headlines are bearish. Pessimism becomes unanimous. Insiders start to buy.
	Extreme Lowest	— 0 —	Extreme Lowest.

▶ Fear and the Unknown

People who are easily frightened invariably have a hypersensitive imagination. If they are superstitious enough to believe in ghosts, let us say, they are quite likely to see apparitions on dark and lonely nights. But if they could summon the courage to touch these feared objects, or even to approach them, they would find them to be harmless domestic animals, or rocks, or posts. As soon as identification has been made, fear will vanish as quickly as did the apparition. Fear stems from the unknown, which appears in the mind as having the ability to harm. It freezes all reasoning powers. But when the unknown becomes *known*, fear usually vanishes and reason returns again.

The same psychology prevails in the stock market, where the tendency is to fear anything that cannot be identified, and which threatens to harm the general market, or an individual stock. When fear overrules reason, the impulse is to sell stocks, regardless of prices, and usually at bottom prices.

But when the mysterious factor responsible for mental panic is unmasked and found to be less harmful than was supposed at the moment when stocks were being dumped, then those same securities will recover again, probably as rapidly as they fell. The lowest prices during a break induced by fright are always reached just before the unknown becomes known, when the dark and foreboding objects which prompted the selling have been identified as light-colored, friendly bodies.

Whatever is anticipated of a pleasant or bullish character is rarely fully realized—especially when it entails something expected to lift the price of a stock. Because the exact nature of the anticipated favorable event is unknown—and therefore mysterious—the moment it loses its mystery that stock is almost certain to react.

A person who understands the law of cycles has much in his favor. Fear can find no place in that person's mind, because a sure knowledge of the intimate relationship between the known and the unknown is already imbedded there. Every triumph of the mind over fear thus tends to multiply the habit of courage and produce success.

▶ The Distilled Waters of Mammon

But the human mind is one element in speculation that is always fixed and will never change. Of course, the majority is willing, if not eager, to invest in stocks almost regardless of prices when the market is having a splurge and everybody is making money. But the real test of character that separates the men from the boys in Wall Street is when those same stocks shrink in value, not just from their bull market highs, but often to only a fraction of the original purchase price.

Because the market always anticipates the future and has proved its forecasting ability many times, some people tend to regard a sharp drop in the market as an automatic harbinger of a business recession, or even a depression. This holds true sometimes, but not *always!* Industrial depressions may result from financial panics, yet again they may not.

▶ Don't Push the Panic Button

A financial panic is sudden and disturbing. A mental disorder, it feeds on fright and usually is short-lived: one deep thrust with a rapier and out again. It hurts many speculators; it squeezes the holders of borrowed funds; it burns up paper profits by the ream. But panic is a temporary disaster: once fright has been allayed, the wounds heal rapidly.

A depression, on the other hand, is an obstinate, malignant malady. It grows quietly and slowly, increasing in scope and force and doing its lethal work often against a background of generally favorable business conditions. It may endure one to three years; but, if caused by a financial panic, it is usually of short duration. A really prolonged depression stems invariably from something more serious than just a drop in the stock market; it means that the intrinsic fault lies within the economy.

Financial panics and industrial depressions are both calamities, to be sure; yet they do not resemble one another, except as they affect business. The influence of a depression is much more lasting than a panic. It harms those who wield the tools that produce our basic wealth and resources. It creates losses that cannot be recovered any more than lost days or hours can be saved. A panic causes losses too and is damaging while it lasts. And if business is already depressed for deep-rooted reasons when a financial panic strikes, the recovery will probably be slow and tedious. But if business is good and a panic erupts, then the latter's influence will probably be only temporary. Witness the favorable performances of both the stock market and business after the 1962 panic spent its force.

Panics have occurred in the past without producing a depression, and the latter has also taken place without the former's help. Yet the average person is always ready to nail the responsibility for a depression on the door of a panic, because panics are flashy and more emotional. They make a much deeper impression on the public mind.

According to Charles H. Dow, founder of the *Wall Street Journal* and father of the Dow Theory:

> The business community has a tendency to go from one extreme to another. As a whole, it is either contracting business under a belief that prices will be lower, or expanding under a belief that prices will be higher. It appears to take ordinarily five or six years for public confidence to go from the point of too much confidence, and then five or six years more to get back to the condition of hopelessness.

▶ Strong Hands—Weak Hands

The alternation between hope and despondency is an underlying cause of market cycles. The efforts of buyers and sellers to anticipate rising prices gradually causes the demand for securities to be artificially enlarged beyond normal investment requirements; it finally results in substantial quantities of stock being accumulated. By that time prices have passed far above their average normal stage. Buyers at these inflated levels are generally less shrewd and wealthy on average than are the sellers. Thus, with stocks being transferred gradually from strong hands to weak hands, the vulnerability of the market increases, until some heavy blow to sentiment (like the steel price hassle in 1962) trips a landslide of selling.

▶ How Now, Brown Dow?

In Dow's day before the turn of the century, the market was much less regulated than it is now. There was no "foreign situation" to be reckoned with, taxes were trifling and no rule limited short selling. High carnival prevailed on the Exchange. Indeed, the sympathy between stocks was so remarkable that any determined group of bulls or bears could drive prices skyward or hammer them lower, just by concentrating attention on a handful of key issues. This made it relatively easy for them to call the turns.

▶ Forecasting Methods

But cyclical studies are infinitely more complicated today; there are so many constantly changing factors to take into account. Also, the rise in popularity of a game called *Beating the Market* has necessarily boosted the number of systems, theories and other methods of trying to do so.

In addition to the famous, though rather antiquated, Dow Theory of interpreting market movements, the following are among the most popular: Hi-Lo Index; Advance-Decline Line, Breadth of Market Index, Elliott Wave Principle, Odd-Lot Index, Dual Market Principle, Barron's Confidence Index, Low-Priced Stock Index, Buying Power vs. Selling Pressure Index, Relative Price Action Ratio and the Dow-Jones 200-Day Moving Average. Other data which avid market students cull for clues to the next intermediate market trend include: "Insider Transactions," referring to the number of shares bought or sold by corporate officers, directors, or major stockholders (over 10 per cent) of a company's stock; "Broker's Free Credit Balances," which show the amount of money standing idle in brokerage accounts; and "Short Interest," which reports the total amount of stock held in the short account, as of the fifteenth of each month.

In addition, many individuals watch ten-year cycles, calling for a decline during the third year of each decade, cycles which anticipate lower prices in the sixth or seventh year, and others that forecast a downtrend developing during the ninth year. Devotees of shorter term cycles, such as 20-hour, 84-hour and 17-week, are also numerous. There is even reported to be a Diamond Theory, which forecasts market movements by the variety and number of hits poled by the New York *Yankees.*

▶ A Pod of P's

The market actually resembles a pod of peas: no two of them are exactly alike, no two speculative moves are ever the same, no two important traders ever operate in the same way. But if you understand that cycles will normally recur and study their characteristics, the market will prove itself also to be a Place where the Power to Pick and Purchase the Proper stocks will Produce Profits for Patient People.

In other words, you must get to know yourself; know your subject; know your objective; and know how to apply this knowledge.

TOPICS:

- Stock market cycles compare roughly with cycles of prosperity, recession, depression and recovery in business.

- There are three phases above normal and three phases below normal in an ordinary market cycle.

- There is a tendency in the stock market to fear anything that cannot be readily identified, and which threatens to harm the general market, or an individual stock.

- Many people believe that a bear market is automatically forecasting a business recession, or even a depression.

- Financial panics and industrial depressions are both calamities, yet they do not resemble one another, except as they affect business.

- Dozens of systems and forecasting methods are in use today.

RULES:

1. The market moves in definite cycles of distribution, decline, accumulation and advance.

2. The demand for a particular commodity, no matter how great or prolonged, will eventually exhaust itself.

3. If you wait too long to buy, until every uncertainty is removed and every doubt is lifted at the bottom of a market cycle, you may keep on waiting . . . and waiting.

4. When fear overrules reason, the tendency is to sell stocks indiscriminately.

5. The lowest prices during a break induced by fright in the market are always reached just before the unknown becomes known.

6. The influence of a depression is more lasting than a panic.

7. The alternation between hope and despondency is an underlying cause of market cycles.

8. No two markets are ever alike; no two speculative moves are ever the same; no two important traders ever operate in exactly the same way.

Chapter 5

It Was
Ever Thus

A WOMAN asked a broker how to go about saving and investing money to give her independence in old age. The broker told her that, by stinting herself over a period of years, she might be able to save about $20,000 before the age of 55.

This at four per cent would give her only $66 a month, which wouldn't be enough to keep her. He therefore suggested that she not try to save much money, but buy cosmetics and chic clothes and make herself so charming that some Adonis with wealth would be sure to marry her and then she needn't worry. The stock market is not the only sensible outlet for investment funds.

▶ Big Booms

Each boom experienced since economic life began has been bigger and better than the preceding one. With our wealth increasing, living standards going up and the population steadily rising, there is no reason to doubt that the next period of economic and stock market growth will be grander than the last.

Yet anyone who believes that learned bankers, brokers, businessmen, or government leaders have discovered a way to perpetuate prosperity, or prevent recessions, had better latch onto a history book. It will temper his optimism during prosperous times and curb undue pessimism during times of stress.

▶ Nothing Is Permanent

It is a great mistake to think that existing conditions will be permanent. After the market has been pummeled by great waves of liquidation and a period of inactivity sets in, we find it hard to believe that it is a prelude only to greater activity again at rising prices. Conversely, when stocks are kiting high and the situation is good all around, we tend to believe that certain factors, which have been "built into" this boom, will make it different from any other and give it an assurance of permanence. Prosperous times are attributed to one set of factors, just as recessionary periods are caused by another set. The majority of us probably can name and describe most of them. But the one fact pertaining to all conditions is that they will change.

▶ Spare That Tree

Prosperous conditions are about alike, just as recessions are basically the same. If a declining market didn't indicate some privation and hardship, the failure of the majority to recognize and take advantage of such regularly recurring phenomena would be almost comical. When everything is bullish we are apt to think: "The tree will grow right up to the sky." When times are bearish, we seriously wonder if the same tree has any cord wood value.

Neither robot computers nor human economists can control booms and busts, yet we are forever naive and credulous in assuming that "the situation is different this time." We thus inherit most of the same headaches, disappointments and assorted financial ailments as people the world over have experienced since man first realized the necessity of a medium of exchange and invented money.

▶ The Charleston Era

To be sure, the stock market is constantly changing; and we are right in saying that it doesn't look the same today as yesterday, or as it will tomorrow. Many of the principal items responsible for disturbances in the past—such as margins and short selling—are more strictly controlled and, of course, the market is bigger and broader. Also, we obviously have learned a great deal in the 30-odd years since the era of jazz and flappers, bathtub gin and ballooning stock prices ended in the speediest, most ferocious and far-reaching crash in stock market history. But in spite of all our experience and newly developed machinery, nothing has been invented to change the faulty reasoning processes of human beings.

One of our thorniest economic problems today is not how to maintain a rate of steady growth in the economy, but how to find a way to make stocks sell for what they are worth and stay there. Yet so long as the Stock Exchange is the world's greatest auction center, where buyers and sellers of securities can meet together on equal ground, the rise or fall of prices will always remain subject to psychological whims and fancies.

A Wall Street veteran, comparing the present with the years prior to World War I, when bucket shops, bear raiding, corners, manipulation and a host of other assorted evils (now taboo) were recognized adjuncts of the brokerage business, would obviously notice many changes.

▶ Then and Now

For one thing, there are no latter-day J. P. Morgans, "Bet A Million" Gateses, or Edward H. Harrimans. The modern market leaders are not single individuals accustomed to swinging hundreds of thousands of shares around as part of their usual routine, but a growing combination of traders and investors known as the public. Through the efforts of the Stock Exchange and its Member Firms the public's participation in financial matters has increased commensurately with its education and interest in them.

Today's market is far too large for any one person, or group of people, to exert more than a transient influence. Not only has legislation, and other steps taken to eliminate unscrupulous operators, been very helpful in this respect, but more shares are listed; stock dividends, mergers, new financing and stock splits have sharply boosted the number of shares outstanding of many companies. Moreover, "dollar cost averaging," or dealing on the installment plan (MIP), has attracted a large following of small traders and investors, whose transactions form an important and expanding percentage of the total turnover.

▶ Who Pipes the Tune?

It is nonetheless a fact that all important markets have a central or controlling force. Before 1900, the trusts and large individual traders set the pace. In the 1920's and in 1937, the public got star billing. During the last bull upswing, pension and mutual funds, savings banks and other institutional investors piped the tune, and the interest of labor unions in the market has burgeoned steadily.

Since the support provided by institutional buyers during the May-June selling stampede of 1962 helped stabilize the market and spark a recovery, the question naturally arises if a second 1929 is possible with this kind of sponsorship in the background.

Of course all things are relative and there are obvious similarities between today and 1929. But history proves that the stock market and the economy are loaded with surprises anyway, and neither one adheres to any rigid set of rules.

The spring 1962 drop was triggered apparently by a sizable number of long-term investors suddenly deciding to convert some substantial paper profits into cash. When the public became frightened, the selling snowballed. Liquidation from margin accounts was not the main culprit; nor was it possible to blame important selling on the funds.* Indeed, as pointed out in the previous chapter, a market panic is simply a natural event that takes place occasionally when a seemingly immovable object becomes suddenly too tired to hold back an irresistible force.

▶ St. George and the Dragon

It wasn't just the fact that stocks dropped, dropped, dropped all along the line that disturbed many people so much as the failure of someone-anyone to put a finger in the dike. For some time we had believed rather complacently that 1929-model panics, or any panic for that matter, had been relegated to the past. In the public's view, St. George was never so marvellous against the Dragon as various agencies and committees have been in plugging loopholes revealed by the '29 blockbuster and introducing new theories and stabilizing methods designed to prevent a repetition of that great catastrophe. Without them the spring slide of 1962 might well have been an avalanche.

To be sure, certain glamour stocks had frolicked unchecked toward greatly overvalued levels long before the main cable snapped, and plummeted the Dow-Jones Industrials through their psychological support barrier indicated around the 700 area. But

* Cash investors were buyers on balance during the three heaviest days of surging trading and wide price swings in May 1962, when 40 million shares changed hands. Although margin customers were net sellers, only about 2 per cent of the dollar volume of all transactions involved securities sold to meet margin calls from Member Firms. Sixty-seven per cent of all short selling during May 28-31 was by specialists in connection with their stabilizing functions. According to the Stock Exchange, the "major impetus" for the heavy selling and buying waves during the period was supplied by individual investors, for whom 673,000 separate orders were executed.

the point is that, regardless of who did what to whom and why, and notwithstanding all the built-in stabilizers, the fine harvest of corporate earnings reported for 1961 and the first quarter of 1962, or the rainbow-tinted forecasts emanating from Washington, the market clearly demonstrated that when the time came for a change of trend it could still go down with a very resounding thud.

A whole new class of traders and investors lost much confidence along with some money, in more or less the same fashion as did their fathers, grandfathers, and perhaps even great-grandfathers, during various sweeping panics that have punctuated our economic life since 1720-1724, when the collapse of the South Sea Company in England and John Law's Mississippi Company in France touched off the world's first great financial catastrophe. Surface appearances may be different today, but human emotions are always constant. It was ever thus!

▶ Do Something, Somebody

To imagine that Washington is going to step in and "do something," whenever the stock market's knees get wobbly, is nonsense. Government relies upon business, just as business depends upon government. It is in the best interests of both to get along amicably. But, as we have seen many times, it is unwise to bank exclusively on help from Capitol Hill and, especially, to gamble hopefully on the possibility of such help forthcoming. In some instances, even when sympathy has been expressed and reassurances given—remember Mr. Hoover's remarks during the Great Depression—they failed to halt the pessimism more than temporarily.

▶ The Funds

Another fallacy is to suppose that mutual funds are always going to "save" the market by supporting key stocks on any reaction. True, the funds and various institutions have ample reserves for investing in selected securities when the moment is appropriate.* But this carrot-on-the-stick situation can endure only for so long as new sales of the funds exceed the redemptions. If cancellations top sales for any length of time, the fund managers will be obliged to join the selling side. It is erroneous to suppose that they can remain impervious to gyrations in the stock market. Moreover, a person whose portfolio consists only of mutual funds will be just as ready to sell them in a time of stress as he would any listed stocks.

▶ "Buck Rogers" Stocks

Finally, it has been almost traditional in Wall Street to assume that a bull market cannot end until the low-priced "cats and dogs" have had a whirl upstairs. But this no longer is true. For one thing, the public has more expensive tastes and is far more discriminating about what to buy and what to avoid. For another, the high-flying "Buck Rogers" issues, which travel five or more points in a day and might also be candidates for a stock split, are much more in vogue. The public currently seems to think that most stocks in the lower-priced echelons are on the wrong side of the market tracks.

▶ Pied Piper of the Market

Security fashions are changing constantly, the same as clothing, hairdos and automobile styles. After the turn of the century, 50 per cent of all stocks listed were rails, and transactions in them constituted a whopping 75 per cent of the total volume. However, in 1928, the market was virtually dominated by utility and industrial issues and it was popular to say: "As Steel goes so goes the market."

U.S. Steel is still one of our foremost industrial enterprises, yet its influence on the price action of other stocks has waned con-

---

* Stock Exchange members and institutions tended to take the buying side when individuals were selling during the late May 1962 market break and the selling side when they turned to buying.

siderably. As a matter of fact, many blue chip members of the old aristocracy—United Fruit, Pennsylvania Railroad and Allis-Chalmers, among others—have also lost much of their former luster. Even the most casual observer must have noticed how badly many of the old-time market bellwethers have fared recently, while relatively new stocks in new industries occupied most of the limelight.

Some stocks retain their market leadership for many years, mainly because their reputation is good and their corporate managements are capable. Yet there may come a time when they no longer grow commensurately with past performance. After reaching certain price levels, they seem to roll over and just "play dead." Traders and investors must watch for this and try to ascertain if the quality of the stock and its future outlook have been impaired in any way. In the market place there never has been any lack of vigorous young princes waiting to be crowned when one of the old kings dies.

▶ Composite Market Picture

Stocks may be divided into five broad categories:

1. Seasoned, "big name" issues, representing the elite of American industry, whose dividends and earning power are unquestioned.

2. Secondary issues, the pale blue chips of younger and growing corporations that have not quite yet demonstrated their ability to withstand competition under certain conditions with the same finesse as older and more established corporations.

3. Relatively new, unseasoned stocks that still must demonstrate dividend stability and earning power. The market needs further time to appraise their potential value.

4. Stocks that have been rolling slowly downhill, and whose chances for regaining their diminishing prestige and market status are very slim.

5. Penny stocks that cannot even pass the listing requirements of an exchange. Most are virtually worthless.

▶ The New Concept

All new businesses and industries must pass through various stages of development before they become established. The more people attracted to them the greater the competition will become. Profit margins tend to narrow and weaker companies are forced out, causing lower market prices for their representative stocks.

The methods of appraising securities have also gradually altered. Where yield was once the principal yardstick of market measurement, so now do analysts tend to consider a stock more on a price/earnings basis. In the future, undoubtedly some other approach will become more fashionable. But any mode of evaluation must be able to look ahead and should take into consideration other well-known appraisal methods. To have any merit it should include some forecast of longer-term prospects for the company and the industry to which it belongs.

▶ Growing Pains

In addition to yield and price/earnings the growth outlook must be considered. In effect, what are its possibilities in the years to come? The income derived from most growth equities is relatively small; sometimes no dividends at all are paid. But so long as longer-range prospects seem reasonably bright, most typical growth fanciers appear willing to forego any immediate benefits. As E. H. Harriman used to say: "I am not interested in ten per cent, I want something that will grow."

▶ Sorcerer's Tools

Through merger, acquisition, or their natural product mix, most corporations have some element of growth; the fruits of research are tending to improve this all the time. Imagine the widespread use of atomic power for commercial purposes; also, the sorcerer's tools provided by automation and electronics. What vast reshuffling will take place in the food industry, when wood is converted into food; when fruit, vegetables, meat, or flowers, can be kept fresh by a split-second bombardment of electrons? Mull over what the harnessing of solar energy will mean, and how the fast-unfolding wonders of the space era will affect our daily lives.

▶ Stars of the Future

Many stocks that will command a place in tomorrow's galaxy of market stars cannot be accurately measured now. The atomic-electronic-space age will surely produce a trunkful of new and dynamic leaders in fields that are still relatively unknown. But investment and speculative opportunities in these growing giants, whoever they are, will still be recognized by basically the same methods as should be always employed when evaluating any stock. They include a study of its technical position, a careful analysis of all news and rumors pertaining to it, a close appraisal of the basic statistics and, especially, the control of various psychological factors which prompt a person to act unwisely.

Economists, financial services, traders, speculators, investors and brokers somehow appear to be almost surprised when they describe today's market as being "new." With more listings now than ever before, another type of leadership in force and a more efficient and knowledgeable class of broker having seized the reins of operation from the Old Guard, of course the market looks different.

▶ So What Is New?

These innovations, plus the complexities of foreign and domestic politics and the cold war situation, obviously have compounded the difficulties of investing and speculating wisely. But to believe that the modern machinery for processing securities transactions, the newer methods for analyzing stocks, the growing wisdom of the public and Wall Street's better-educated and -trained personnel are going to maintain booms and prevent busts, or even make the average person recognize their periodicity so that he can really capitalize upon them, is all wrong. The stock market may have changed superficially, but its constantly conflicting price trends are based on shifts in public opinion.

The market actually is very old; only we who participate in it are new!

TOPICS:

- There are other sensible outlets for investment funds besides the stock market.
- To suppose that booms can be made permanent, or recessions outlawed, is to overlook the lessons of history.
- A big problem today is not just how to maintain a rate of steady economic growth, but how to find a way to make stocks sell for what they are worth and stay there.
- The spring 1962 drop was triggered apparently by a sizable number of investors suddenly deciding to convert some substantial paper profits into cash.
- Without new theories and stabilizing methods introduced by various agencies and committees over the years, the 1962 market slide might well have been an avalanche.
- Stocks may be divided into five broad categories.
- Most corporations contain some element of growth.
- Stars of the future in the market galaxy.

RULES:

1. Each boom experienced since economic growth began has been bigger and better than the preceding one.

2. The one fact pertaining to all conditions is that they will change.

3. All booms are about alike and recessions are basically the same.

4. The rise or fall of prices will always remain subject to psychological whims and fancies.

5. All important markets have a central or controlling force.

6. If cancellations top sales for any length of time, mutual funds will be obliged to join the selling side.

7. Bull markets do not necessarily end with a final whirl in the low-priced stocks.

8. Security fashions are changing constantly.

9. The market's constantly conflicting price trends are based on shifts in public opinion.

The Malady

Chapter 6

The Trader's Trilogy

1. Vanity

PROBABLY the greatest single enemy to stock market success is vanity—one's own personal vanity. It is vanity that leads us to take small profits, but large losses. Even a fraction of a point net profit is all right, because small as it is, you have nevertheless beaten the market and that is a sop to vanity. But a fractional loss hurts your pride and, instead of accepting the loss after a stock begins to act poorly, you decide to wait for a rally to bail you out.

► Say It Isn't So

To take a loss is to confess that your original judgment was wrong; and that is not nice to admit. You hate to have your friends know you were a victim. Worse, you shrink from having yourself know it. Unconsciously, a man may say to himself: "I'm going to make up that $100 loss, even if it costs me $1,000." While you are waiting for your stock to recover, it sinks to a point where the facts are too painful to face. You don't sell then until your broker almost demands that you sell.

In the board room of any large brokerage firm you will see a number of men sitting around, calm and collected. Most of them probably have tiresome losses to which they have long become accustomed. They are still hoping to appease vanity by getting out even and are prepared to wait. On the other hand, if you see a nervous, fidgety man, evidently not quite sure what to do, he probably is trying to make up his mind to sell and thus clinch a small profit before his vanity is in jeopardy.

An active trader, when going over his records, will sometimes observe that the majority of completed transactions were profitable but that, paradoxically, his total losses exceed his profits—simply because nearly every loss is large, while most of the profits are small.

Because of vanity, men hate to be *compelled* to do anything. They refuse to concede that even a price slide in the market, with perhaps a margin call from the broker, or a banker's demand for collateral, can make them sell an issue they hadn't planned to sell. Hence, they will strive mightily to meet the call, when swallowing pride a little sooner and taking a minor loss would have avoided most of the trouble.

▶ Turning the Other Cheek

It is vanity also, which makes the majority of people in a declining market buy *more* of the same stock in which they took a licking. Amateur traders who average down in an overvalued stock when the market is trending lower don't lose so much on what they buy at first as on what they buy later to try and even up.

Instead of quitting when the stock is obviously headed lower and switching into another issue that seems poised for an advance —or staying out of the market entirely for a while—they say to themselves: "I'll teach that stock a thing or two; it needn't think it can throw me for a loss." The weaker the stock is, the more they seem inclined to buy as it slips downward. They return to kiss the hand that struck them!

It is partly vanity that makes some men buy on margin, since, by that method, they may purchase 100 shares of a favored issue when they actually can afford just an odd-lot. They do this because the number of shares they can buy outright seems too trivial.* Unable to deal in stocks on a grand scale themselves, they feel woefully small as they see thousands of shares passing on the ticker tape. Yet the truth is that the average person in the market doesn't have many hundreds of shares.

▶ **Snow Job**

Perhaps it is vanity too that makes a man believe the bullish story he hears about a stock. Everyone likes to be behind-the-scenes, an insider, and when he is told in strict confidence that such and such, now selling at 40, will go to 60 because of an impending new development, he is inclined to believe it. Except for vanity, men wouldn't pay so much attention to supposed inside information, but the greater a man's vanity, the more positive he is of his shrewdness in acquiring such information, and hence he is just that much more likely to hold on longer and perhaps lose more. The more thoroughly he believes the bullish story, the more he seems willing to risk. If the stock reacts suddenly at first, he plunges in deeper, expecting that certain secret plans he has heard about will soon bring a turn in his favor.

Even if the plans concerning which he had intimate knowl-

* No one knows how many consumer goods sell for a high price largely because a high price is demanded. Almost anybody will agree that if the best quality diamonds should ever become so plentiful that they would bring only 30 cents a carat, nobody would wear them. And it is equally probable, if the manufacture of imitation diamonds became so expensive that the imitation cost more than the real, that a great many persons would discard the real for the imitation. Vanity would make them want to show the world proof of their ability to have that which costs the most—a visible symbol of achievement; just as the Indian warrior wore scalps in his belt to show what a mighty man he was.

edge were true, they may have gone awry—as plans often do. But the speculator whose vanity gives him sublime faith in something he has heard usually fails to use his reasoning powers and check more thoroughly on the story, until some of his capital has gone "where the woodbine twineth."

2. Greed

Next to vanity, the greatest foe of good judgment that anyone in the market must guard against is greed. It is wise to let profits run and follow a stock with Stop Orders in an uptrending market. Yet if people became more accustomed to selling stocks at the prices they first expected, their position would be improved considerably. Many a time a person will enter an Open Order to sell a stock at a stipulated price and then, when the stock approaches that price, cancel the order, because he decides that a few hundred dollars profit isn't nearly enough. Almost always, whenever an individual thus cancels an order he placed before greed got the upper hand—and then ignores the protection of a Stop—the stock goes down and is finally sold below the figure that he first planned to accept.

Sad words are these: "Oh, if I had only sold when . . ." But we all use them. Because we have our share of human greed, it is always more difficult to make up one's mind to sell than to buy. It is a fact that not one-tenth as many people will take warning and get *out* of a dangerous market, when urged to by someone in whom they have faith, as would follow that same person's advice on the buying side.

▶ Market Glutton

The explanation is that you buy because you see a chance to make money; but when you sell you abandon the present hope of further gain. Nobody likes to place himself in such a position, does he? Thus it appears that greed is a more powerful influence than danger. People are so optimistic by nature that they are not easily scared. Beautiful as is optimism, we must beware of it. As P. T. Barnum observed: "Not every optimist is a sucker, but most suckers seem to be optimists." The optimist always expects that the market will move upward soon. But once fear has been induced, it works much faster than enthusiasm.

Maybe one reason why many financial services and market letter writers so frequently favor the buying side is not merely because they themselves are naturally optimistic, but because their readers anticipate such advice. Their greed makes them almost eager to be told to buy. If a stock market forecaster predicts an advance that doesn't come his followers will forgive him. But if he turns bearish prematurely and warns of a slump, his reputation may be shattered. Greedy people who sold on his advice before the peak is reached will never forget the money they think they might have made.

▶ **Let Her Eat Cake**

At the spring 1961 top of the bull market in the electronics group a young lady asked a friend what one glamour stock would merit a $2,000 play.

"Invest your money in a steady dividend payer representing sound value," he told her, "or go on a trip to Europe. No one can take that away, but if you plunge into some high-flying stock, selling at 50 or 60 times earnings, you may lose part of your capital."

And lose is exactly what she did. She needed to preserve her capital and she craved a trip to Europe, but greed made her try to have her cake and eat it too.

The worst losses in the market come naturally from uninformed people buying greatly overvalued stocks. The surprising fact is that people actually buy such stocks knowing full well that they are probably too high, but expecting to resell them to someone else at an even higher price.

If everyone followed the advice of some astute investors, who commit themselves in the market only two or three times a year, they might benefit substantially in the long run. However, practically no one would believe such advice, no matter how often it was given. Few can sit back and wait for reactions. Greed is the enemy of patience. You should guard against the buying fever; it is a dangerous disease.

3. Hope

After vanity and greed, perhaps the worst influence on anyone trying to make a profit in the stock market is the "will to believe." We think to be true whatever we *hope* is true. When a reputable doctor tells a man he has an incurable disease, the man is then liable to fall into the hands of some quack, who says *he* can cure him. The patient ordinarily would pay no attention to the quack, but now if he doesn't believe him, his only hope is gone.

Likewise, men pin their faith on poor stocks and expect them to advance, because therein may lie their last hope of financial salvation. When a man is most confident that a certain stock will climb, what he really means is: "Oh, if it only would!" His confusion and maladroitness make him hope when he should fear and fear when he should hope. He is virtually unable to grasp the fact that to buy cheap and try to sell dear is often to sell cheaper. Trained analysts who work studiously in the research departments of large brokerage houses are qualified to give expert advice, well mixed with caution. Yet many individuals are too stubborn, or impatient, to heed their counsel.

▶ On Burning Paper Profits

A broker friend tells this story about a client who had a small fortune in paper profits in a leisure-time stock. In his imagination, he had already spent the money putting the down payment on a house, buying a new car and taking his wife on a long-promised holiday. While reviewing his position one weekend after the stock had been under pressure for a few days, he found that his $20,000 profit had shrunk to $17,000. Now, even $17,000 dropped into one's lap out of the stock market isn't to be sloughed off; but having once mentally spent the $20,000, he didn't like the idea of readjusting his sights to a mere $17,000. So he quickly convinced himself that the drop was only temporary; that the stock would recover again, giving him back the full $20,000 and perhaps more besides. To back up his opinion he decided to buy more of the same stock, so that even a small advance would return to him the original profit.

But the stock staged only a "soda-pop rally" before resuming its decline. The man now found that he must have far more stock than before to regain his $20,000 on an average recovery of one or two points. That $20,000, although only on paper, had become as real to him as if it were actually in his pocket; and his imaginary expenditures, particularly those for pleasure, had become so much a part of his way of life that he thought he simply *had* to have the money.

Acting contrary to his broker's advice, he bought more of the same. The fact that the price had dropped so sharply should have been indication enough that something was wrong somewhere in the picture. But the man's vision was completely obscured by paper profits, which by this time had contracted to $3,000. An acquaintance suggested that he get out of the stock entirely, instead of waiting for a mere two or three points recovery, and exchange it for something else with better appreciation prospects. In other words, the man was easily talked into buying an even more speculative issue. Now in the mood to grasp at straws and believe almost anything, he was lucky to close out eventually with about $1,100 of his original $20,000 gain left intact. He was another victim of the "will to believe," who discovered too late that cold facts are seldom as sensational as unchecked imagination.

▶ Castles in Spain

Hope only obscures or warps one's judgment. It increases the possibility of loss. It is a flashing red light in the trader's pathway. Because intelligent speculation must be based not on desire, but on careful analysis, you should make it a rule to get out of the stock market, or an individual stock, and avoid danger whenever you find yourself hoping. Our innately deceitful human qualities tend to make us believe what we want to believe, rather than what is so, and to prefer to hear what is pleasant, rather than what is true.

The author of the following lines may never have owned a single share of stock, but the idea behind them might well be emblazoned above the entrance to every board room in the country:

> Hope tells a flattering tale,
> Delusive, vain and hollow.
> Ah, let not hope prevail,
> Lest disappointment follow.

TOPICS:

- Vanity is the single greatest enemy to stock market success. It makes some men try to average down in a poorly situated stock; others to buy on margin and still others to believe a particular bullish story they have heard.

- Another foe of good judgment is greed.

- When a man is most confident that a stock is going to advance, what he means is: "Oh, if it only would."

- People are so optimistic by nature that they are not easily scared.

- The "will to believe." Cold facts are seldom as sensational as unchecked imagination.

- We think to be true whatever we *hope* is true.

RULES:

1. It is always more difficult to make up one's mind to sell than to buy.

2. Greed seems to be a more powerful influence than danger in the stock market.

3. The worst losses in the market come from uninformed people buying greatly overvalued stocks.

4. Whenever hope becomes a chief factor in determining a market position, sell out promptly.

Chapter 7

The Insiders

*To speculate in Wall Street when you
are not an insider is like buying cows by
candlelight.*   —DANIEL DREW

PEOPLE who operate in the stock market
may be divided into two general classes: those
possessing the right knowledge and psychological attitude, the so-called insiders, more popu-
larly referred to as "THEY"; and those known
collectively as "The Public," who lack much
training and are further handicapped by temperament.

The public, dealing in relatively small lots,
are substantially more numerous than THEY; but
despite this apparent advantage, they tend to
buy the wrong stocks most of the time, buy the
right stocks at the wrong time, fail to exercise
enough patience in holding the right stocks, or
shy off taking profits in issues that seem fully
valued and susceptible to a price correction.*

* The latter is due in large part to the capital gains tax penalty and/or to
human greed, which prompts a person to hold on stubbornly for the "last ⅛ point."

▶ **A Tricky Trio**

Before the 1930's, the rightfully skittish public regarded THEY as an evasive and shadowy all-powerful group, operating ghoul-like behind the scenes, with all the experience and low cunning of a Daniel Drew, the forcefulness and conceit of a "Jubilee Jim" Fisk and the shark-like strategy of a Jay Gould. Whenever a stock, or group of stocks, rocketed suddenly straight up, or thudded lower with awesome force, it was automatically assumed that THEY were buying or selling in huge blocks.

But, since the advent of the Securities and Exchange Commission, the identity of THEY is much better established.*

▶ **The Cast**

First come the bankers, corporation directors and executives, the trust officers, the managers of large institutional portfolios, pension funds and others, who help to formulate economic history and usually have access to advance information. It is generally conceded that they are the leaders of the modern market.

Then come the big individual operators, who usually are not members of any exchange, but are apt to take a major position in one of several stocks when their inside informational sources suggest that the time is ripe.

Next are the so-called professionals—thoroughly experienced individuals, operating as floor or office traders—who base their commitments on a variety of fundamental, technical and other market factors, such as tape action, volume considerations, sponsorship, earnings, yields, and changing business and international news developments.

Finally, we have the semi-professionals—not necessarily members of the brokerage fraternity—who concentrate their full-

---

* Testimony to the interest in stocks today: The British Reuters will arrange with Americans on safari in Africa to furnish them, via radio, with stock quotations. Also, an Akron, Ohio, bistro installs a stock quotation board for cocktail hour customers. Pert models, in short shorts, do the board marking.

time efforts on buying low and selling high. Depending upon the individual's ability in the market and his financial acumen and connections within the business, he may be one of the public, or even one of THEY.

▶ Goldfish Bowl

The insiders naturally wish to keep their stock market intentions secret for as long as possible. However, the SEC now requires the directors and officers of any company whose stock is listed on a national securities exchange to file a monthly report showing: (a) All purchases or sales of their company's stock made during the previous month; (b) The total number of shares held at the end of the month. A similar report must be filed by the owners of more than 10 per cent of a stock registered on any exchange, and all indirect holdings must be made known.

Coupled with information published regularly by various funds, showing what positions in securities have been initiated, augmented, or eliminated altogether, it is now possible to know what market action the directors, officers and other large stockholders of various companies have been taking, and what specific stock groups and individual issues have gained or lost favor with institutional investors.*

▶ "Guesstimating"

No one need be a complete "outsider" any longer, yet there still is no direct pathway to the inside. By the time the nature and extent of the preceding period's insider transactions are published, some of the data may lack much significance. Consequently, the pastime of "guesstimating" what THEY are doing *now* is still as popular as ever.

---

* An example of well-informed buying by THEY was the 10,000 share commitment in E. F. MacDonald Co. made by the Madison Fund during the second quarter of 1961. Putnam Growth Fund later took on a 29,600 share block and Massachusetts Growth also climbed aboard with bundles of 13,500 and 23,500 shares. Compared with a price of 19, when the stock went public in 1961, the bid price soared above 130 late in March, 1962.

It is a strange fact that almost anyone, especially the man sitting next to you at the broker's office, will volunteer to confide exactly what THEY *are* doing. But it is doubtful, indeed, if any other subject produces such vast stores of misinformation.

To the average person, THEY are giant striding men, unusually gifted in foresight and omniscience, who have a magic wand for prodding market prices upward or downward, whenever the moment seems timely.

One board room trader whispers to another the name of a stock.

"THEY are getting into it," he says. "It should be good for twenty or thirty points. Better get aboard."

At the word, THEY, the other trader has pricked up his ears.

"Is the stock being accumulated now?"

"Sure. It's apt to move any time."

Even the biggest and most successful professionals do not have 100 percent infallibility. When they win in the market it is not entirely because they have inside information about a particular stock but perhaps because they have learned by experience and observation more about crowd psychology than the general run of speculators. In other words, they are able to anticipate what thousands of others in the market are most likely to do and to act beforehand.

▶ Selling on the Decline

These shrewd professionals learned long ago that, because man is by nature a bargain hunter, it is relatively easy to sell him stocks when prices are declining.

But most of us in our zeal for bargains are poor judges of bargains. People remember a stock's former high price, long after they forget that it also had a former *low* price. We may think a stock is cheap simply because the price is lower than it was yesterday, disregarding the possibility that it may be still lower tomorrow. Wise men do not buy a stock until it has been through severe tests and shown an unwillingness to go any lower. Yet we are often too impatient to wait for a stock to show its mettle and, consequently, we are a great help to THEY.

We see a stock climb from 65 to 88. Each time it registers a little higher than it has been before we wish we had bought it sooner. Our mind is inclined to assume that whatever has been happening will continue to happen. Hence we decide that a stock that has been on the upgrade will keep right on in the same direction. We are greatly assisted in this belief by rumors that THEY are planning to take or increase a position in it.*

► Specialty Stocks

Whether the basic price trend is up or down, Wall Street at all times is subjected to a continuous bombardment of information regarding the general market, a group of stocks and specific stock issues—particularly "special situations." This data appears in different forms. It may have been derived from contact with a corporation official, or gleaned from the spring crop of annual reports. It may take the form of a news dispatch given out to the press, or a speech presented before a group of security analysts.

► Courting Miss Fortune

Because the market feeds on news and "inside" information and fluctuates according to their changing character, it is essential that traders and investors be able to distinguish between real information, based on legitimate facts, and "dope," which has been manufactured from the most flimsy material and, in many cases, is pure fiction woven within the recesses of a wild imagination. Real information can be invaluable in wooing Lady Luck, but dope can lead only to an unhappy union with Miss Fortune.

---

* Any extraordinary movement in a stock will usually spark rumors about a split, a merger, or some other sensational development about to take place. The move will probably continue for a while, pending an official confirmation, or denial, yet the impact of *either* possibility upon the market should be studied closely.

The confirmation of a rumor will generally spark profit taking and thus bring an end to the move. On the other hand, should a denial be accompanied by just a minor reaction on diminishing turnover in the stock, with only a relatively small portion of the preceding gain being lost, the setback may be technical and chances are good that the previous trend will soon be resumed.

In the midst of this bouillabaisse of facts, news, views, rumors, tips and gossip, it is very easy indeed for the unsophisticated person to become hopelessly confused. What then should be his attitude? Should he ignore the data completely? Surely nobody would recommend such drastic action. Nonetheless, he had better do so if he is going to accept such a welter of facts and fancy at face value.

▶ Need More Than Just Statistics

A pinch of common sense used while seriously considering all this should help him determine what his attitude will be about the problem. It would naturally be easy to make money in the market if all one had to do was take advantage of the near, and sometimes not so near, information that spreads every day through the financial district like measles in a boarding school. Likewise, if stocks moved up or down solely on the basis of background statistics, one's chances of becoming a millionaire would improve considerably. You would only have to estimate with fair accuracy what so-and-so might be going to earn, what yield the dividend would provide, what its industry status was and so forth, before projecting a price for the stock. When it approached that price, you could sell out, pocket the profit and simply repeat the process. But even the greatest novice must know that no such easy road to riches exists anywhere.

▶ Naïveté

The main trouble with anyone who is at all addicted to tips, rumors and the like is his childlike innocence in believing that the particular one that he has just heard is bona fide, and he accordingly plunges in with little thought of the consequences. He knows that most tips are worthless, but is willing to take a chance. Vanity, greed and hope thereby combine to push him along the road to financial suicide.

When you trade in the stock market you depend on information. Some sources are reliable, some rumors are well founded and a tip occasionally does make good. So the problem whittles down to your ability to distinguish between information based on the granite of true facts—for which there is really no substitute—and that which is supported only by wild overenthusiasm or unfounded gossip.

▶ Rifle Versus Shotgun

A trader's mental attitude should be always receptive, open to conviction, but not gullible. When information is received, regardless of source, examine it under a microscope. By keeping abreast of the general business trend, political developments abroad, the basic factors underlying various leading industries, the technical price pattern of the over-all market—as well as your favorite stocks—*and* by effectively squelching the mental gremlins that continually try to influence you toward unwise decisions, you should be able to form a fairly accurate opinion of the information you have received and the wisdom or foolishness of acting upon it.

▶ Corporate Nabobs

Perhaps the natural thing is to question an officer of a successful business enterprise for information about conditions in and prospects for his own company. Here, surely, one can get information from the fountainhead and it cannot well be wrong.

THEY, the officers and directors of a corporation, from their inside vantage point, obviously should know more about their business than any outsider. They know at all times whether their corporate ship of profits is on or off course. They know too if cost-cutting methods are effective, if new products are being well received, if profitable markets are opening up. They have the pole position on all questions about dividends, stock splits, mergers and the earnings outlook.

▶ Laying It on the Line

Indeed, since they have at their fingertips nearly all the inside facts that an actual or potential stockholder would most like to know, their own purchases or sales of their own stock represent highly worthwhile information. People may talk about what they would like to do, but what they finally do, in putting their money on the line, so to speak, is really what counts. For example, if you find that corporate insiders have been consistent sellers of their own stock, it would be wise to overlook any favorable rumors or tips that might be circulating.

▶ The Forest and the Trees

It is nevertheless true that many company officials and directors are notoriously poor judges of the stock market. To be sure, they know earliest of any new developments taking place within the company. But this inside knowledge does not mean that they are equally wise and well informed about the market action of the stock concerned. A corporate insider, perhaps because he is "too close to the forest to see the trees," may be prejudiced about his own company, just as a mother has biased opinions about her children. He is too much on top of the proposition for his judgment to be always at the best. When business is prosperous, he is optimistic; when it is booming he is enthusiastic. But when business is not so good, or in the doldrums, more often than not he is likely to be overly pessimistic.

On the one hand, his self-interest may compel him to think too highly of his stock. On the other, because he may have sold some or all of his holdings too soon, he may speak disparagingly of the future. Perhaps if he thinks of buying in again, he may express himself in not too optimistic terms, or even view the future somewhat gloomily. He is certainly honest in all he says, yet his stock market point of view may be influenced by personal prejudices. "The biggest bear is a sold out bull." Moreover, no matter how truthful his statements may be, they may lead one astray; there is always the danger of buying the stock at the wrong time when the public is not in a buying mood. Whenever there are more sellers than buyers then the price will drop, no matter how good a stock may be.

► For God, for Country and for Company

Corporate officials are generally men of strict integrity and high ideals. But they are also businessmen—first, last and always. Ordinarily they do not trade in and out of stocks, and are far more interested in the conduct of their business than how the company's stock is doing in the market. Very often they may not even be able to tell you at what price the stock is selling.

Their usual policy is merely to submit the facts as they see them and let other people form opinions about their significance. By applying your knowledge of the market to the statements thus released, you should be able to determine with fair accuracy whether it is a proper time to buy the stock, or sell it.

However, because some officials may unconsciously make statements that sound biased to fast-acting traders, all such reports, oral or written, bullish or bearish, should not be swallowed without a good deal of chewing.

► Founding Fathers

Professional insider buying is generally more significant than the selling.* This applies particularly to companies that have grown large over a period of time, enabling various founding fathers to build up a rather substantial position in the stock through splits, options and dividends. In order to put their estates in a liquid enough position to meet inheritance taxes, they may be obliged to steadily reduce their holdings in the company; such

---

* During a hectic three-day trading period in late May 1962, the insiders—mainly officers and directors of listed companies—bought 5½ times as much stock in their companies as they sold.

sales do not necessarily imply any lack of faith in the future. Indeed, consistent long-term investment purchases made by relative newcomers to the same company's ranks may almost simultaneously offset sales being made by the older officials. If this be the case, such as with large companies like U.S. Steel, or General Foods, insider transactions would be practically meaningless, as far as the market prospects for that stock are concerned. More significance should therefore be attached to the smaller companies.

▶ From the Horse's Mouth

One does hear, occasionally, of inside tips connected with professional operators, who are nearly always successful, and it might be wise to follow them. However, by the time you hear that a professional operator is buying on a grand scale, the chances are that he may actually be selling. If he were buying, come to think of it, he wouldn't be advertising his actions, any more than a man who wanted to buy a horse advantageously would go around telling how much he admired it.

▶ Professional Honor

It is nonetheless fair to add that any truly successful stock market professional presumably has enough self-respect and pride not to wish to lead others into disaster. He does not wish them to assume risks that he himself may take. One such person, who sold out his position near the peak of the December 1961 market, had several friends following his advice. But, while he himself was making money, most of the others lost. Yet his intentions were the best. True, they didn't lose much. He was so afraid his friends might lose that he advised them to buy only the safest, most conservative securities. But they were so conservative that they didn't fluctuate much in either direction and therefore did not offer much profit. Consequently, they were neglected and dropped somewhat in value. In other words, the price the man's friends paid for insurance against losing much was to lose a little.

▶ More Than One Broker

When THEY begin to buy, the operation is often conducted through several brokers. The result of such purchases soon begin to show up on the ticker tape, where it is seen by all those who pay close attention to price movements. Moreover, once it has appeared on the tape, it is printed on the financial pages of newspapers. These factors are observed instantly in all parts of the country by credulous traders, who begin to exclaim: "Look at that. There's evidently something doing in National Hotdog. It's being bought in big lots. Must be about to have its move." Then the general public reasons: "THEY are buying in big blocks. The insiders know that a rise is coming. Let's buy now before the real advance starts." They overlook the fact that when the public begins to crowd one another and bid aggressively for a stock, the price will naturally spiral.

▶ Buying Easier Than Selling

Amateur traders are always saying that this stock or that hasn't yet had its move, implying that sooner or later it just naturally must move upward. Indeed, their confidence almost suggests that there are laws, rigidly enforced, which require that every stock on the board must sell at higher prices when its turn comes. The real explanation is that, whether in the stock market, or elsewhere, we are always expecting the things to happen that we hope will happen. It is not surprising that amateur traders usually buy more readily than they sell. Since everybody is looking for profits, it is natural that people are prompt to accept the first sign of higher prices as a signal to buy.

When little stock is in the public's hands, that stock is said to be closely, or strongly held, or in a "good technical position." But if the public is loaded up with a certain stock, then wise observers say that, while it may be intrinsically good, it is weakly held and its technical position is poor. "Too much stock is hanging over the market." At such a time prudent operators aim to let that stock alone. They prefer to wait until the public has tired of it and sold.

▶ The Shakeout

Two methods are readily available for dislodging stock from so-called weak hands: by scaring it loose and by wearing it loose. In other words, we may be frightened into selling when we shouldn't, due to fear of a possible loss, or we may sell simply because our patience is worn down. After holding a stock for several months in anticipation of a rise that fails to come, it is natural to think: "That doggone stock is never going to move. I'm practically even on it. I might as well sell and put my money into something with more life."

▶ On Selling Too Soon

Astute professionals have learned by experience and observation approximately how long human patience can hold out in a given market situation and are sometimes able to capitalize upon it. The length of time required to discourage those who are holding an inactive stock often runs from four to seven months—occasionally even longer. During that time the stock usually looks and acts just about as unattractive as it possibly can. Thus it happens that while many traders lose money by receiving information too late, many others lose also by having the information too soon and selling out in disgust, perhaps right on the eve of an important rise.

▶ The Public's Holding

A statistician in New York once made quite an exhaustive study, stretching back over a period of years, which showed how much stock of the various corporations in which he was interested was held in public hands. By his observation, not only of these figures but of accompanying market performances in the past, he was able to estimate with some confidence that when the public holding of a given stock was above a certain point (which point his experience enabled him to recognize), then the stock would have difficulty moving upward.

While he was reluctant to disclose the exact method by which he arrived at his conclusions, the statistical student nevertheless did reveal a possible short-cut method by which one might be able to detect too heavy public holding, just by studying the newspaper reports of market transactions:

> One may at least be fairly sure that when a stock climbs briskly several points higher than it has been before, and then *stays* at or near that high point, the public is sure to buy it and hold it until they finally change their minds about its being ready to go still higher.

▶ Playing Possum

When the papers are full of reports about a certain industry being in a thriving condition, the public may rush in and buy stocks in that industry, and such public holding is the very thing that may prevent the stocks, during several weeks or months, from fully responding to good news about that industry.

If you held a good stock for a long time, but finally grew discouraged because it wouldn't advance and sold, then the stock was almost sure to take a sudden interest in life once again and start sensationally upward. While you held on it was just playing possum.

▶ Don't Be Just Average

The explanation is simply that a normal person has just an average store of patience and hence we all behave about alike. When you and I become wearied from holding a stock that seems hopelessly disinclined to come up to our optimistic expectations, and tell our broker to sell, it is almost certain that hundreds of other holders in the same impatient mood are likewise selling. Closing out our position at the wrong time is the penalty we pay for being just average.

▶ The Stretch

When attempting to accumulate a block of stock in the open market, the professional buyer may methodically bid just so much each day and rarely a fraction more. If the buyer is willing to pay 40 a share for whatever stock is offered, he limits his bid to 40, or below, and pays no attention to offerings at 40¼. In the language of Wall Street, he does not *reach* for stock. However, there may come a time when he may suddenly and unexpectedly bid a point or so higher, depending upon how he applies his knowledge of mental processes in the human animal.

If you are seated in a broker's office day after day, scanning the cryptic hieroglyphics of the ticker, and surveying a great area of blackboard representing the ever changing prices of various stocks, you may observe some morning that a certain stock, long quiet and selling within a narrow price range, has suddenly become active. Not only active, but at sharply advancing prices. Each sale of several hundred shares is a fraction above the previous sale, and after only a few minutes, the stock sells two or three points higher than it did when this brisk little movement started. Then prices recede slowly once more and perhaps after an hour the stock is quiet again. Probably the best price you could obtain, if you try to sell, is about the same that has been prevailing for the past several days.

▶ Tickling Your Vanity

Here is one explanation: experienced traders, who are aware of the mental hazards that afflict most of us, know that the average man likes to tickle his vanity by getting a little better price for whatever he has to sell than other people are getting. When a stock has been dawdling for a long time invariably around 40, a number of holders of the stock are liable to say to themselves: "I'm not going to sell at 40, but I'll take 41." Others may put their selling prices at 41½, or 42. They don't wait until the stock is selling at the higher figures before they try to sell, but place their selling orders in advance with an admonition to the broker to "Keep Them Open!" These Open Orders may be on the specialist's book for weeks before they can be executed. Perhaps the total number of shares thus offered is not worth thinking about, but to an institutional purchaser, or market professional, who wishes to buy a block of the stock in the open market and has noticed from recent action that there seems to be a temporary ceiling over it, the number may be important. Accordingly, one day, when the stock is lolling around 40, the broker may be instructed to buy all that is offered up to 42, or to buy a specified number of shares with 42 as the top limit.

▶ Soda-Pop Rally

This brings about a sudden run-up, somewhat suggestive of a mouse darting out of its hole after a cheese niblet and right back into its hole again. The stock springs forward suddenly to 42, let us say, and then (unless the full number of shares specified in the 42 limit order has not yet been acquired) it promptly begins to recede. If the enterprise were not quickly carried out, many who had sell orders entered between 40 and 42 would change their minds and raise the price. A few traders, noting that the stock recently loafing at 40 is now at 42, offer their holdings "at the market," that is, for sale at the best price immediately available. But to their great disgust, the price has probably sagged back close to its original level by the time their orders are executed.

One may properly be suspicious of a stock that pops to a new high when most other stocks and the general market appear to have already reached their probable peaks. The chances are that the price of the stock is not based on any overnight improvement in the company's position, so much as on the new buying stimulus provided by overenthusiastic individuals who believe it is "behind the parade" and due for a run-up.

But, on the other hand, when a stock sells higher than it has before, or at any rate, the highest in many months, near the *beginning* of a bull market—that stock will bear watching and should probably be bought. The price is much more likely to represent genuine value than at any other time. To begin with, just after a long decline, and before a new bull market has gained headway, most speculators haven't much money. When other stocks have thus been drifting aimlessly, trying to find their own levels, the behavior of a stock that forces its way up may be significant. If it can spurt upward that way counter to the trend, or in a dull and lifeless market after a decline, then it probably will go much higher when the whole market is ready for a broad and sustained recovery.

▶ The Slowpokes

Reversing the situation, when a stock of superior merit goes down gradually of its own weight, or under an onslaught of selling such as occurred in the spring of 1962, it may be slow to come back—much slower than many inferior stocks—simply because it often will lack the stimulus of sudden short covering to bring it back. Only a very few sold it short for the reason that the merit of the stock made the practice too dangerous. Someone may notice that a stock declined only a few points from its former high, compared with the deep setbacks experienced by other stocks, and say: "It behaved so well that it must be good. Hence it will snap back rapidly. I'll buy it for a quick move on the rally." But it will probably recover just as slowly and sluggishly as it went down.

▶ Tough Sledding

The first few points of recovery by a stock after a long period of dullness are sure to be the hardest sledding. This is because a multitude of people who bought it at slightly higher prices, and have been disappointed, are anxious to get out even, and are quick to sell when their original buying price is reached. So heavy is the stratum and so much stock must be absorbed at every step, that it sometimes seems as though the entire issue is being offered for sale at every ⅛ point up.

▶ Running the Shorts In

But it usually happens that after the first difficult three- or five-point rise, the next several points are negotiated with surprising ease. The explanation is that once the stock has broken out of its bottom range of accumulation, it begins to attract more traders who, believing it was a false breakout or that the price has advanced far enough and what goes up must come down, begin to sell it short. This creates an artificial but sure demand for the stock as the advance continues; market bears are easily alarmed and some of them decide to buy back almost as soon as they have sold short. Then, since people always prefer to buy during an advance, the brisk activity of the stock at higher prices attracts still more buying.

Conversely, when a stock drops sharply on heavier volume to its lowest price in a long time, but during two to three months thereafter fails to go still lower, then it is probably going, not lower, but higher—after sufficient reaccumulation has taken place.

▶ Take a Number

Nearly everyone who operates in the stock market has his own theories and ideas about how to "beat it"; and most of us subconsciously have definite number habits that enter our thinking processes. Ask anyone suddenly to write down a number between one and ten and the chances are two out of three that he will write seven. For some unknown reason, seven is the favorite number with the majority of us. Likewise numbers ending in five and zero are handy numbers. Our preference for them probably goes back to the days when we were learning the multiplication table and found that we could use multiples of five much more rapidly than other numbers.

According to Census figures, there are more people aged 35 than either 34 or 36, simply because it is easy to say 35 to the census taker for any age near that figure. Judges sentence many men to ten years in prison, but few to nine years. Even wage scales show the influence of the numbers habit. A man rarely receives $66 a week, yet he often receives $65, or $70, or $67.50, which is a compromise between two multiples of five.

▶ Hi-Lo

Now, these same number habits are often felt in stock transactions. If you look at a newspaper giving the high and low prices of all stocks on the New York Stock Exchange for an entire year, you may observe a surprising number whose annual high was a figure ending in a four, or a nine; in other words, just under a multiple of five. Stocks generally make a high price of 124 or 149 far more often than they reach 125, or 150. The reason is that we think in round numbers and try to sell at a round number, but don't always succeed.

▶ Buyers Versus Sellers

Imagine a room with buyers on one side and sellers on the other side. Most of the sellers are asking, let us suppose, 150 for a stock, but the best bid is only 149. Finally, enough sellers decide to take 149 to fill at least part of the demand. Then the price drops to 148 and lower. All who held out for 150 now wish they had accepted 149. Some traders in the market are clever enough not to wait for round numbers, but to sell ahead of the price that the majority will ask.

Nearly always when a stock moves through 100 for the first time it immediately carries higher, because considerable pressure was required to push it there and the momentum of carrying the stock through that level is likely to carry it a little further.

Reversing the process, the low price of your favorite stock for the year is fairly certain to be just above a five or a zero. More stocks sell down to 91, or 101, than go to 90, or 100. We say of a favorite stock: "If it goes back to 90, I'm going to buy it." But more experienced buyers may get in ahead by bidding 90½, or 91.

If you had a neighbor in the grocery business who tried to sell and make a profit on goods that would disappoint customers, you would probably hold such a fellow in contempt. He would have a hard time staying in business. But operators in the market don't deal directly with the other party and don't even know who they are.

▶ Who Gets the Blame?

The truth is that every one of us who deals in the market tries to follow the same technique of buying cheap and selling dear. And we do this with no intention of being unfair, or harming anyone to whom even a small loss may mean hardship. As a matter of fact no one should speculate in the market unless he can *afford* a loss. Those of us to whom the loss of a few hundred dollars is vital haven't any business to be in the market at all. Many of the most speculative and dangerous advances are made not because of THEY, but when the uninformed public gets excited and bids a stock up, thinking not of its yield or value, but only that it might sell higher tomorrow. When the realization comes suddenly that the price is too high, then a sharp drop, cancelling several previous days of laborious gain, may occur in a single session.

Professional traders, floor specialists, corporation officials, institutional investors, indeed, anyone and everyone who might possibly be linked with THEY, then get the blame when our own avarice and vanity are the only true culprits.

TOPICS:

- THEY versus The Public.

- Who are THEY?

- Securities transactions by so-called insiders can no longer be kept secret.

- The general public's inexperience and naïveté about market matters are frequently very helpful to THEY.

- Many successful market operators are also clever psychologists.

- The changing character of the news background which influences action in the stock market.

- How valuable is the information received from corporate sources?

- Professional insider buying is generally more significant than the selling.

- How THEY operate. Weak hands and strong hands. Stretching the public's patience.

- Some technical factors underlying the rise and fall of prices.

- Our subconscious addiction to numbers habits.

RULES:

1. Never buy or sell merely on the basis of background statistics. Technical market considerations and psychology must also be taken into account.

2. Don't believe everything a corporate official says about his company's stock.

3. Check over all the facts carefully yourself and view them conjunctively with other known market factors.

4. Just because the general market is strong, it does not mean that everything will be strong. Nothing requires that a certain stock, or group of stocks, move upward simultaneously with the others.

5. After a stock has gone through a long period of price accumulation, then suddenly becomes stronger on heavier volume, carrying through the top of its trading range, it bears watching.

6. Many stocks reach their highs for a move just under a multiple of five. Low prices for a move are likely to hold above five, or zero.

7. Never speculate with the money you need to live. If you can't *afford* a possible loss, stay out of the market.

Chapter 8

Blondes
and Bonds

NEAR the end of the question-and-answer period at a large oil company's annual meeting recently, a lady in the back of the hall raised her hand. When recognized by the chair, she got to her feet and asked for a portable microphone.

"Mr. President," she began, "one thing has bothered me since I became a stockholder of this company. Whenever you put up a gas station on the street corner or anywhere, how do you know you'll find oil?"

The question naturally broke up the meeting, and it may be a long time before that lady summons the courage to ask another. But those in the audience who laughed loudest and longest should be reminded that women and finance only recently became acquainted.

Men have the least right to be critical if women are short of financial knowledge. The latter may justly claim that men have endeavored to keep them so; for the lords of creation have regarded this particular field as exclusively their own domain. Says the *Harvard Business Review* on the subject: "There is no minority group against which there is a greater discrimination than women in business." "Stags Only" signs on the Executive Suite and the frequent inconsistency of wage scales between the sexes seem to bear this out.

▶ How It All Began

The ballads of early England describe how the greatest ladies "Plied in chariots daily, or pawned their jewels for a sum to venture in the [Exchange] Alley." But economic suffrage was slow to develop. Before the coin of our realm was distributed by death and taxes, the role in life for women was largely economic and based upon holding the family together by providing food, clothing and shelter. The Heroine of the Household was actually the "family labor." She was typically a timid soul, with few outside ambitions and not much inclination or knowledge of how or where to use them if she had.

▶ Ways and Means

In years gone by, the female investor was not actually an investor. She transacted her business solely through an attorney, or some relative, and seldom was even aware of, or cared to know, how her money was put to work, so long as she received interest payments regularly and verbal assurances of the safety of her principal.

But as more stocks were listed and the volume of trading grew, exaggerated reports about killings made in the market began to seep uptown into the fashionable drawing rooms. The infatuation of stock gambling became so intoxicating that more and more women began putting their money into stocks instead of stockings.

They usually engaged some small broker to handle their

business and, having deposited the required margin, would follow the market trend diligently day by day. Unmarried women speculators generally maintained accounts in the names of male friends or relatives. Other accounts standing in the names of women on brokers' books belonged to the wives of active stock operators who recently had made a profitable play. The latter type accounts were set up mostly to insure the family against the inevitable "rainy day"—which dawned quite frequently—when the speculator who had lost everything was obliged to fall back on his wife's money in the hope of renewing his fortune.

▶ **Chivalry Counts**

The ladies came, they saw, and they conquered sometimes in Wall Street. Yet frequently, even when they lost—depending upon the chivalry of their broker (and what broker was so ungallant as to let a lady lose money in his office?)—they nevertheless managed to come out ahead. Sometimes the broker put his shoulder under the load during a panic and saved his fair client. Very often, if the lady's margin was exhausted and her tears were profuse enough, the noble broker would allow the account to travel on a new margin of beauty, grace and smiles.

Women obviously were rather an asset in the social balance sheet of some brokers' lives. But their speculative sorties for the most part were void of real success. They appeared to lack the mental qualities required to absorb the various points of a situation, and seemed incapable of generalizing the factors that tended to affect the market. Elizabeth Cady Stanton and George Sand were among the few who excelled in their own field before branching into speculation. But they were no more outstanding speculators than other average members of their sex, whose market decisions were sparked too often by feminine impulsiveness, rather than sound judgment.

The great exception was Hetty Robinson Green, the celebrated "Witch of Wall Street," whose unaided sagacity placed her among the ranks of successful millionaire speculators. Mrs.

Green, however, was made up of a powerful masculine brain in an otherwise female constitution. She was one among ten million of her sex. But she was always a miser and she never knew much happiness.

▶ Crystal Gazers

If Hetty Green stood alone at the top of the women's financial ladder, Victoria Woodhull and Tennessee Claflin sat on the bottom rung. "The Queens of Finance" were spiritualists, suffragists and advocates of free love. They were also sister-partners in 1870 of the first all-female brokerage firm in Wall Street. The girls knew nothing about money matters: "I have at least one financial opinion and that is that gold is cash," Tennessee conceded during an interview. Yet the girls certainly could change an amorous male into a tangible asset, and the firm endured until the electric pair discovered that spooks, stocks and sex couldn't quite pay the rent. This hard fact of economic life ended women's first real intrusion into the financial arena.

▶ Take Care of the Ladies?

Women today can establish themselves in any business and enter any avenue of life that they are qualified through education to fill. With or without benefit of jobs or wedding bells, they control 85 per cent of the spending power, own 65 per cent of the value of all legacies and deposits in savings banks and are beneficiaries of more than 80 per cent of life insurance policies. By 1970, when female workers will number about 30 million— an increase of 25 per cent over 1960, versus a 15 per cent gain for the males—their stock should be stratospheric and a strong bull market in chivalry will really be underway on Wall Street.

▶ The Ladies Can Take Care of Themselves!

New industries and labor-saving devices, more modern homes with fully automated equipment and other marvellous inventions just coming to light have enabled the hand that rocks the cradle to switch to signing checks. A great deal of this newly earned or acquired money has been invested already in blue chip equities. "Les Girls" outnumber the male holders of American Telephone & Telegraph two-to-one, they represent 57 per cent of the 594,976 individual holders of General Motors and they number 78,203 at Consolidated Edison, against 45,480 men.

Most women are long-term investors. They are not much concerned about daily or weekly price variations. However, there are also many others who prefer to trade in the market. Not only are they occasional traders, but they are frequent and daring speculators, often taking risks that would appall the oldest market veteran, or rushing boldly into situations where even a Rockefeller would fear to tread.

▶ Doing What Comes Naturally

It is natural that wealthy women with plenty of leisure time or working women with money lying idle in banks or savings accounts should think about the stock market. It matters not who spark such thoughts—husbands, brothers, relatives, or friends— the fact remains that there are no more eager or venturesome gamblers in Las Vegas or Monte Carlo than women, and there are no more avid or audacious speculators in stocks than women.

Speculation requires fortitude and patience which are, or should be, womanly virtues. Speculation derives its food from excitement and women often feed on excitement. Speculation comes from fancy and women are much given to fancy. Indeed, women of a certain type are naturally, or by education, very much inclined to speculate in stocks. Some speculate to augment household allowances, others to stretch small salaries, or restore take-home pay to its original amount. And there are countless women too—perhaps all, if the truth were known—who have a secret inborn hankering to beat men at their own game.

The Wonderlic test of intelligence indicates that college women are smarter than men. Moreover, the ladies have proved themselves to be whizzes at managing household pennies, and they frequently pull down big salaries. There is no logical reason why they shouldn't be equally adept at the intricacies of speculation. But despite these factors, which suggest that women are almost ideally suited to be market operators, there are no present-day Hetty Greens and no female has shown the true Midas touch.

▶ Lady Be Good

To be sure, many women with ample funds and sources of information are probably as justified in taking a "businesswoman's risk" as the average knowledgeable businessman. But their number is relatively limited. Most women are more or less dependent—in many cases completely so—upon income. They should confine themselves to only the safest and soundest securities; there are a thousand ways to go astray financially.

A woman has a friend who made a killing in real estate; another has successfully placed her money in various business ventures; still another has a bonanza in a carefully culled list of common stocks. If her friends have all made money in this way, why should not she? If the particular woman is so situated that she can assume a reasonable risk, she might be justified in taking it; but if she relies entirely upon income, she must first make certain that her principal is secure and that the regularity of interest and dividend payments is assured.

Needless to say, any widow absolutely ignorant of market matters, who does not know the difference between a stock and a bond, is hardly in a position to supervise wisely her husband's estate. Where a widow has the best investment counsel little harm is done. But the large sums which disappear regularly in reckless business ventures show that a diligent study of the elements of investment will repay itself many times in the long run.

▶ Ex-Speculation

Whether a woman has $1,000 or $100,000 to put into securities, she should observe the following:

1. Before investing any surplus funds, make sure that adequate insurance and cash savings are available for use in an emergency.

2. Decide definitely what is required from stocks and bonds, then contact a reputable broker, who will help to formulate a purchasing program.

3. Diversify the available funds in equal dollar amounts among a number of securities. This will have the further advantage, if care is used in selecting interest and dividend payment dates, of providing a steady income throughout the year.

4. Be contented with modest profits, or satisfactory income. The stock market is no place to win a ranch mink in a hurry; anyone who believes otherwise may only wind up pawning the old raccoon instead.

5. Develop a continuing interest and increasing knowledge about securities and, above all, be patient in holding them, assuming that nothing adverse happens in the favorable picture which prompted the original purchase.

6. Review all holdings periodically. A stock may be outstanding for a number of years and then go into a decline. When it seems to have done as well as can be reasonably expected, sell it and switch into something else.

▶ Belles and Brokers

If the average woman chose a broker or investment counselor as carefully as she selected a dressmaker or beauty consultant, both would have more comfort. Women are considered more loyal to their broker than men and are more likely to introduce him to new clients once their confidence has been won. One strange thing about a certain type of woman is that she can't learn anything from other women. Her education, her experience and judgments, her opinions about life, have to be achieved through men. When advice is offered by her own sex, she thinks of it as counterfeit. Fortunately, that type is rare.

It is true, nonetheless, that a great many customers' brokers (registered representatives) of both sexes in Wall Street prefer to handle a man's account than a woman's. Some say this is because women are generally poor losers, and have too many mental foibles to make them amenable to deal with. Others claim that they expect far too much time and service for the amount of business they do.

▶ The Male Slant

When a man loses he either blows his brains out or is philosophical about the loss. He may dislike his broker intensely for what has happened, but after a preliminary outburst—caused by a natural tendency to blame someone else for his own mistakes—he will charge off the loss to experience. But the average woman, who may be already on the defensive, will often create a considerable fuss and blame the broker for everything under the sun. She usually cannot afford to lose the money she has risked through speculative activities, and it will be a long time before she is reconciled to the loss.

▶ The Female Slant

The trite saying, "Them that has gets," is basically true. But it does not follow that those who have the most money, or can get it the easiest, are the best losers. Many women, who cannot afford to lose, nevertheless splash in the stock market. It makes little difference whether it was difficult for them to acquire the funds they are risking in the first place. What makes them such hard losers is the fact that they know their ability to replace what they have lost is generally limited. When a man loses, he knows he can go back to his regular business, earn more money and perhaps try again. But the funds a woman loses very often represent the money she needs to live. She may have no earning power to replace what she has lost, and therefore tends to be a worse loser than the average man. Money is just more vital to her.

A woman is aware that her broker is usually familiar, or should be, with most of her dislikes and preferences about securities and with the current status of her account. Since the broker is in a position to know what many other investors or traders are doing, and works every day close to the golden heap, he can very often supply valuable information to her.

▶ *A Woman's Prerogative*

But one snag is that if a woman knows her broker well enough for him to tell her things in confidence, he also knows— and the woman knows that he knows—exactly what she is doing. Therefore, if she sometimes goes contrary to his advice and follows her own judgment, or a tip, she is almost compelled to be *stubborn* and stick to her mistake, assuming it is a mistake. The woman's *pride* and *vanity* may not permit her to let him see that she knows she is wrong. She will probably adhere to the course

▶ *Double Dealings*

Some women have accounts with more than one brokerage firm and not just a few are maintained primarily to be able to buy or sell contrary to one broker's advice without hurting his feelings.

"About half the time," a woman confided, "when Broker A tells me something he thinks I should do, I know he has unconsciously been influenced by the conversation and behavior of various customers, most of whom are sure to be wrong, so I am inclined to do the opposite from what he says, although in a different office with Broker B, so he won't know that I have acted contrary to his advice."

on which she started in the *hope* that she will be right in the long run. To do otherwise would be an admission that she is not fit for the game.

▶ **Intangibles**

Women have shown that they can invest profitably and wisely, but it may be mostly in the matrimonial line that they are the best speculators. According to the *Ladies' Home Journal*:

• Money, women believe, is something that should be used to beautify something else. A ranch house, the small fry, herself, even her husband. But definitely not the Forty-First National Bank.

• Yet most women know from experience that the "ghost" walks only once a week—on Friday. And that money isn't that green stuff on trees.

• Family advice on how to spend money leaves a woman singularly unmoved.That also goes for anyone who doesn't talk her language: "Bargain"—it might come in handy at the beach; "Little $5 earrings"—$5.98 plus 20 per cent tax; "Savings"—coffee was ten cents off, so that's why we're having steak tonight.

• If there's anything that burns a wife to a crisp, it's having to get a special appropriation every time she'd like a bangle bracelet. What she wants is some none-of-your-business money.

• A man can get stony broke, but a woman can always locate a few dollars in a George III tea-caddy, a mad money locket, or the creases of your favorite lounge chair.

On the other hand, it has been truthfully said that the power of a woman should never be underestimated. To be sure, her economic reasoning—the feminine in finance—often baffles men. But women respond quickly and electrically to ideas that stir their emotions and imaginations. Since they already own the majority of privately held stock and are constantly buying or inheriting more, it behooves all males to consider what will happen when they start counting their stock votes instead of their shares. Men may be living by the sweat of their frau a lot sooner than they think.

TOPICS:

- Women and finance in the early days.
- Hetty Green stands at the top of women's financial ladder, but Victoria Woodhull and Tennessee Claflin sit on the bottom rung.
- The role of women in finance today.
- Most women are long-term investors, but they are also daring speculators.
- Six rules that women should follow in the market.
- The male slant, versus the female slant.
- A woman's prerogative.

RULES:

1. Women should confine themselves to only the safest and soundest securities.
2. It does not follow that people with the most money, or those who can get it the easiest, are the best losers.
3. Before investing, make sure that adequate cash savings and insurance are available; decide what you require from stocks and bonds; diversify available funds in equal dollar amounts; be contented with modest income or satisfactory profits; develop an interest in and an increasing knowledge of securities; review all holdings periodically.

Chapter 9

The Mood
of the Bear

'Twixt optimist and pessimist
The difference is droll;
The optimist sees the doughnut,
The pessimist the hole.

EVERY speculator should know what every keen student of human psychology already knows, that the mass of people are overwhelmingly less intelligent than the few. All scientific intelligence tests—in the army, in schools and colleges, everywhere—indicate that about two per cent of all the people in any community are more capable of reaching wise conclusions than the other 98 per cent.

One can easily prove this by checking over his own list of acquaintances. You probably know at least 30 persons fairly well. Now, of these 30 intimate friends, neighbors and other acquaintances, aren't there two or three who are more sensible, whose opinion you would rather follow than all the rest put together? It probably is safe to say that the judgment of the head of a large corporation about his business is usually worth more than the composite opinion of all his employees. No matter how many people start running around a track, they can't overtake the champion.

Surely it is reasonable to assume that a fairly representative cross section of the public participates in the stock market and, therefore, if the majority of all people is less capable than the few of deciding anything sensibly, this must also hold true of their behavior in stocks.

▶ *Wrong Impulses of the Majority*

We know that a person obviously must buy when prices are comparatively low and sell when prices are higher, or vice versa, to make a profit. But if most people had the foresight to take advantage of low prices and buy, then the low prices would not exist since there would be more buyers than sellers. If the majority were cagey enough to sell the instant that stocks are priced beyond their worth, then peak prices would never be reached. In short, if everybody were truly intelligent, no one would sell too cheaply or pay too much, and the result would be that wide price swings would not occur. Prices would be confined to such narrow limits that no speculator would pay much attention to the market.*

* Come to think of it, a big drop in the price of a company's stock doesn't really represent a decrease in the value of that company, because no considerable amount of the stock could have been sold at the exact top price, and therefore that price never represented true value.

Suppose you are a big stockholder in a company, owning perhaps 20 per cent of the common stock outstanding. You note that the price of this stock has advanced from its original $2 to $10 a share. This, you reflect, makes your holding now worth so much. But you couldn't get that much; for if you tried to sell your block of stock, you would break the price. The best way for you to get $10 a share would be if the stock kept advancing above that figure and you sold a few thousand shares at a time, or you were able to dispose of your block at $10 through a special Exchange Distribution, or a Secondary Distribution.

When IBM was selling at its 1961 high of 607 one might have multiplied that price by the number of shares outstanding and offered the resulting figure as the worth of IBM. But this would have been a fallacious value, since there was no possible way for all the stock, or even a substantial fraction of it, to be sold at the high price.

▶ Look the Other Way

Unanimity of opinion is a dangerous thing; and one way to win in the market, then, is to avoid doing what most others are doing. We may not know what the highly intelligent majority is doing, but by watching and studying the crowd, we can pick up useful clues as to what that same majority is *not* doing. In other words, those of us who are only moderately intelligent and might not behave wisely by independent effort always have the opportunity to join up with the smart folk if we'll consistently pay no attention at all to the signs which say: Follow the Crowd!

▶ What Cooks With the Crowd?

The only trouble with this idea of sometimes going contrary to the crowd is that one must first identify what the crowd is really doing. Besides, it is not so easy as it sounds to perform differently even if one does know; also, there is no use in working doggedly against the market's basic trend—whether it be up or down. But when all our neighbors, our favorite financial publications and all other agencies keep drumming it into us that one line of action is wisdom, such thoughts become so merged with our own that we tend to do what everybody says.

The idea of making money by coppering the bets of the crowd is not, however, a mere theory; for it is precisely what successful operators do on both sides of the market. Men of wealth and wisdom (THEY—the insiders), who have enough important contact with banks and other sources of information to know what is going on backstage, can often determine with an above-average degree of accuracy when a stock, or a group of stocks, seems overbought and a trend change is imminent.

In certain respects, therefore, a person who trades in the market in a small way has great advantages over the big operator. Granted that he has equal intelligence and skill, he can make more money for the amount used, than if his transactions were on a grand scale; for he can buy low and sell high without rippling the market.

When the ratio of new highs to new lows and the index of daily odd-lot purchases to sales are unfavorable and the preponderance of market activity is in low-priced speculative issues, with the trading volume contracting as stocks have difficulty advancing further on good news, these big operators suspect that the market is getting topheavy. They say that the technical position is poor. Especially if this jibes with a deteriorating statistical pattern, it is just the time for them to sell. Not only do they liquidate their long position, they even sell stocks they don't own (sell short), for they know that prices must go down.

▶ **The Short Sale**

The short sale has been called the most complicated of all ordinary commercial transactions. Yet, as applied to stocks, the principles of selling short are but slightly different from buying on margin. When a stock is sold short, delivery is made to the buyer with borrowed stock. When stock is bought on margin, payment is made to the seller with borrowed money. If objection is made to the principle of selling what isn't owned, or in the seller's possession at the actual time of sale, the same voice might well be lifted against the practice of buying something without being able to pay for it.

The seller may remain short indefinitely, so long as it is possible to borrow stock and the contract requirements are fulfilled. No interest is charged on a short position. However, it should be noted that (1) a premium may be necessary for borrowing the stock; (2) the short seller is liable for any dividends paid during the life of his contract; (3) if the capitalization is small, or the stock is closely held, the broker may have difficulty acquiring the amount of stock needed for delivery.*

---

* A condition arising from this is known as a "bear squeeze." When the lenders of stock sense a tightening supply situation, they may be inclined to call back the stock they have loaned. A tightening supply has an upward effect on the market price. Therefore, anyone intending to sell short should first check to find out if enough stock is available to borrow, particularly if the number of shares outstanding is relatively small.

▶ *Modus Operandi*

The method of executing a short sale and the brokerage mechanics involved are always identical—yet the reasons motivating an original selling order may differ widely. Suppose you have unfavorable information about a certain company that makes you believe the price of its stock will sell lower in the market when the news becomes public. Perhaps the dividend will be reduced, or omitted; its sales may trend lower; or a squeeze between costs and prices will depress future earnings. Such factors seem to represent grounds for "bearishness" (pessimism) on the future market price of the stock of the company concerned. The way to capitalize on this adverse news is to sell the stock short.

In this instance a sale is being made for speculative profit. The transaction constitutes a private venture and involves no regular species of security business. Short sales of this type are made usually by broker-members of the Stock Exchange, or customers dealing through Member Firms, who sell short for a "quick turn" over a period of hours, or days, or as a longer-term speculation.

▶ *Methods of Operating on the Short Side*

Other types of speculative short sales are made rapidly and often, but for relatively small profit, by so-called professionals during the course of their daily business. Considered as contributing to a more orderly and liquid market, they include short sales made by (1) the specialist who, in his dual capacity of broker and dealer, must maintain a firm and continuous market in one, or a limited number of securities; * and (2) the in-and-out floor trader, whose rapid and frequent dealings on the long or short side of the market make for closer, more stable prices.

---

* The most significant aspect of the biggest one-day drop in the stock market since 1929—September 26, 1955, following President Eisenhower's heart attack—was not the $13 billion decline, but the specialists on the floor of the Exchange, who put up $100 million to $300 million of their own money to prevent catastrophe. Had they not taken this risk, the drop might have reached $26,000,000,000.

However, it should be emphasized that not all short selling is speculative. Some short sales represent insurance against large price fluctuations. Others may constitute a temporary condition for facilitating the regular flow of securities owned by the seller. They are essentially technical in character and should be distinguished from the more speculative types described above.

▶ Selling "When Issued" Stock

Sometimes when old securities are made exchangeable for new, as the result of a stock split, a stock dividend, or a merger, the new certificates are not immediately available in deliverable form. Without recourse to the short sale, the investor might not be able to liquidate quickly the "when issued" certificates to which he is entitled, but has not yet obtained.

Although the sale of "when issued" stock is not a short sale in the strictest sense (because it does not require borrowing stock for delivery), it nevertheless involves the sale of property which is not yet actually in the seller's possession, and is therefore termed a short sale.

▶ Selling Stock Obtained Through "Rights"

To protect against the possibility of a price decline before the new stock made available by "exercising rights" is obtained, individuals sometimes sell short in advance the new stock to which they are entitled. Having sold this stock and borrowed the same amount temporarily for delivery, the seller finally closes the contract by returning to the lender the new stock when he obtains it from the issuing company.

Both these examples differ from other general types of short selling in that no necessity of repurchasing the securities sold short is involved.

▶ Selling Short for "Hedging" Purposes

Used primarily as insurance against large price fluctuations is the short sale for hedging purposes—sometimes known as "selling against the box." It entails selling short an amount of stock which is equivalent to the amount actually owned.

Because a long and a short position in the same number of shares of the same stock is maintained simultaneously, profits are fictitious. Any profit gained through price appreciation of the securities owned is cancelled automatically by a corresponding loss shown for the same securities, which have been sold short, or vice versa. Moreover, dividends are nullified, since payments on owned stock revert to the lender of the borrowed stock.

Selling against the box is conducted often by investors who may be undecided about the intermediate price trend and wish to stay on the sidelines until the market outlook is better clarified. Whereas hedge sales could formerly be used against short-term profits for tax purposes, legislation has now blocked this loophole.

Hedge sales are also important to the "Odd-Lot Dealer" (a broker operating in 1-99 share lots), who must avoid a large position, either long or short of the market, and to the arbitragist, who capitalizes upon varying supply and demand conditions by buying a stock in one market and selling it in another. Likewise, to the "Put and Call Dealer," who arranges contracts whereby the holder may demand (Call), or deliver (Put), a certain amount of stock at a specified price, on or before a fixed date.

▶ **The Unpopular Bears**

Despite the legitimacy and practical necessity of short selling, stock market bears have sometimes been regarded as "charter fifth column members, working subversively, overtime, against all the holders of long stock." This opinion has resulted mainly from stories handed down about former use of the short sale for manipulative purposes, and how the practice furthered sleight-of-hand trading methods in the old days.

Stocks invariably go down faster than they go up, and a month or two of plodding advance by the market can be cancelled in a couple of days of brisk selling. This, plus the fact that the bears can make money while the bulls are losing it, doesn't sit well with the latter, who supposedly outnumber their adversaries better than ten-to-one.

Moreover, an extended bear market implies lower earnings and dividends, falling prices and hard times ahead. Since Americans are basically optimistic, the paradox of trying to profit by a decline in values is naturally suspect and generally unpopular.

A combination of these factors caused the short sale to be considered the Big Board's prime instrument of perdition for many years. This was true especially during periods of depression, when stocks were barreling over the falls. At such times, with evil motives being ascribed to all short sellers, serious efforts were made to curb or ban their activities.

▶ *Anti-Short Selling Legislation*

The first important law against short selling was enacted in 1610 by the Amsterdam Dutch. In 1733, "Sir John Barnard's Act" prohibited use of the device in England, while Napoleon I banned all Frenchmen from selling short in 1802.

A decade later in this country, the New York State Legislature also outlawed the short sale. Although similar measures were adopted in Tokyo, Berlin and other financial centers, they were soon rescinded. None of these laws accomplished their primary objective. Without the stabilizing influence of the short sale and its covering purchases, there was nothing to brake the booms in the market or support the breaks.

On the London Stock Exchange, for example, some of the worst declines occurred, not in the speculative issues, but in bank stocks, where short selling was prohibited by law.

Only three times since 1858, when the initial ban was lifted, has short selling been impossible on the New York Stock Exchange: (1) for ten days in 1873, when all dealings, long or short, were suspended to allay the panic; (2) in 1914, for 4½ months, when war in Europe caused a similar closing; and (3) for two days in September, 1931, when short selling was prohibited as an emergency measure, after Britain quit the gold standard and European securities collapsed.

But anti-short selling legislation has been futile and all investigations or studies on the subject have been inconclusive. In 1907, because of the panic, a committee was appointed to investigate operations on the New York Stock Exchange. Following is part of their report relating to short selling:

> We have been strongly urged to advise the prohibition or limitation of short sales, not only on the theory that it is wrong to sell what one does not possess, but that such sales reduce the market price of the securities involved. We do not think it is wrong to sell something that one does not now possess, but expects to obtain later. Contracts and agreements to sell and deliver in the future property which one does not possess at the time of the contract, are common in all kinds of business.
>
> The man who has sold short must some day buy, in order to return the stock which he has borrowed to make the short sale. Short sellers endeavor to select times when prices seem high in order to sell and times when prices are low in order to buy, their action in both cases serving to lessen advances and diminish declines of price. In other words, short selling tends to produce steadiness in prices, which is an advantage to the community.

More recently, in 1951, the Twentieth Century Fund compiled a study on the subject, which summarized: "In the twenty years since May, 1931, there appears no conclusive evidence that short selling materially affected the extent of a major decline or a major advance in the market as a whole."

▶ Some Famous Bears

Credit for inventing the short sale, as applied to stocks, belongs to Jacob Little. A pioneer in an age when gambling and manipulation were recognized parts of a broker's calling, Little reaped a fortune selling short in the panic of 1837. Although later outdone in scope and ingenuity, many of his tricks served as models for stock market intrigue in the 1860's. But, like most bears, Little overstayed the market and sold the Erie short too often. In 1856, unable to hold the line with 100,000 shares short of Erie, he failed for $10 million.

Also meeting disaster via the short selling route was Daniel Drew, Wall Street's *Ursa Major* of the Civil War period. His famous couplet—"He who sells what isn't his'n, must buy it back, or go to pris'n"—carries a solemn warning for all stock market bears. But the Great Bear somehow forgot even his own warning. When Drew died in 1879, his sole assets were a Bible, a watch and chain, a worn sealskin coat and a stock ticker. Liabilities, on the other hand, totaled over $1 million.

▶ No Secrets Allowed

Fortunately for us, the devices used by many famous and some infamous bears to win renown and occasional fortune are no longer permissible. Under SEC supervision, the short sale as a bludgeon in the hands of the speculator is entirely a reminiscence. Indeed, regulations such as the "⅛ Rule" make it impossible.* Secrecy, the gambler's former ace-in-the-hole, has been trumped by a decree that original selling orders be marked "Long" or "Short," and by a rule requiring regular monthly publication of short selling figures. Higher commission rates, the capital gains tax and strict margin and loan requirements have further curbed the speculator.

▶ Good Old "Teddy"

The role of the bear in maintaining a broad and stable market is nevertheless important. Because he can close his contracts only by purchasing the securities he has sold short, the bear is a potential buyer and a good friend in a declining market. By

---

* In order to prevent short sellers from depressing the market deliberately, the Securities Exchange Act of 1934 stipulates that a stock may be sold short only if the selling price is at least ⅛ point higher than the last "regular way" sale (regular way means not a short sale), or if the selling price is the same as the last sale, if such sale is higher than the last different price of a "regular way" sale.

helping inadvertently to support the market, he is actually creating a demand for securities and assisting the very bulls who may censor his activities. So long as ours is a free economy and selling short for possible profit is legitimate as buying long for the same purpose, there will always be bears.

▶ Honey in Short Supply

But most bears are chronic pessimists, hence they are chronic losers. The natural enhancement of values works constantly against them, and the bull markets last longer than the bear.* As any bear will testify, it is purgatory to be long of stocks in a weak market, but it is hell to be short of them when they rise.

There are myriad other hazards, too, that Bruin must overcome in his quest for Wall Street honey. For one thing, the long-term market trend is basically bullish. Every perpendicular decline or panic in the past has been followed later by a grand sweep upward to new highs.

Another danger is the possibility that a stock sold short will shoot upward suddenly. When a man buys a stock at 50, he knows that the most he can lose is 50 points. But on the short side of the market, the sky can be the limit. The stock may simply climb, climb, climb.† It is perilous also to suppose that seemingly worthless "cat and dog" stocks will go down the fastest in a bear market. Do not forget that dust, feathers and other things with neither weight nor value, rise soonest and most easily.

▶ What Are Little Bears Made Of?

A man's real taste for speculation probably comes after he first buys and sells at a profit. Money made so easily—as it appears,

* The longest bull market was the 1949-1962 model; the shortest lasted a mere 23 weeks from April to September, 1939. The longest bear market endured 37 months from May, 1946 to June, 1949; while the five-month period from November, 1938, to April of the following year was the shortest.

† A famous example is the 750-point vault achieved by Northern Pacific RR in one day during the "Nipper Panic" of May, 1901. More recent, though less spectacular advances were scored in the 1949-1962 bull market by Zenith Radio, Xerox, IBM, Polaroid and many others.

out of almost nothing—with no special labor involved, soon prompts more cyclone action with a view to scalping further gains. Small figures may become large ones; but small profits, in frequent attempts to enlarge them, sometimes become large losses. Now these losses, plus a gradual whittling of margins, soon expand into the notion that the losing side of the market must be the buying side and the selling side the winning side. Because the public is usually bullish and therefore fated to lose, it naturally follows that one way to win a profit is to copper their bets. Moreover, since most people are less smart than a few people, success does seem to sometimes depend on doing the opposite from what they are doing, especially if there is evidence that they are heavy buyers in a market that seems to be making little headway after a long advance. Thus are some bears born.

There are various advantages to this way of operating. Indeed, what better recent proof is available than the mauling the market took in 1962, when the Dow-Jones Industrials lost in six frantic months all that the bullish contingent took three years to gain?

It is nonetheless true that average people go short of stocks with far more timidity than they go long of them. "John Q." is seldom a bona fide bear. He may liquidate his long position and remain in cash, or hold on grimly for an eventual recovery, but he is usually reluctant to sell short. It goes against the grain. Speculation is generally a fair weather pastime, and when the chill wind of a bear market begins to whistle along Broad and Wall, most ordinary people tend to hold aloof.

TOPICS:

- About 2 per cent of all the people in any community are more capable of reaching wise conclusions than the other 98 per cent.
- The folly of following the crowd.
- Professional operators make money on both sides of the market by coppering the bets of the crowd.
- Methods of operating on the short side of the market.

- Anti-short selling legislation enacted in the past has been futile, and never accomplished its primary objective.

- The short sale as a bludgeon in the hands of the speculator is entirely a reminiscence today.

- What makes a bear?

- Average people go short of stocks with far more timidity than they go long of them.

RULES:

1. One way to win in the market is to avoid doing what most others are doing.

2. The method of executing a short sale and the brokerage mechanics involved are always identical.

3. Not all short selling is speculative.

4. Stocks always go down faster than they go up, and bear markets are shorter than bull markets.

5. The role of the bear in maintaining a broad and stable market is very important.

6. Selling short for possible profit is as legitimate as buying long for the same purpose.

7. The long-term trend of the market is basically bullish.

Chapter 10

It's
the Season!

IN the spring, entranced by the analogy of a stock market rising with the sap in the trees, some traders like to anticipate a "Spring Rise." In the autumn, when the leaves are falling, they think in terms of a "Seasonal Decline."

► Stars and Sun Spots

The record shows that there are about as many spring falls as spring rises and as many autumn rises as there are falls. It would be hard indeed to find, in the chronology of market movements, any six-month period when there was not some recovery that could be termed a rise, or a decline that could be called a fall. Yet some people—who should know better—still toss their fortunes in the lap of Lady Luck and base their interpretations of market movements too often on sun spots, the stars, or seasonal factors.

Despite the fallacy of placing such reliance on questionable forecasting methods, the fact that Year-End Rallies, January Thaws, Spring Rises, Indian Summer Setbacks and other phenomena are mentioned so frequently suggests that they have won some credence in some speculative investment circles. The implication is that seasonal factors are dependable and traders should be able to capitalize upon them.

► Calendar Influences

Seasonal changes affect the profits of nearly all industries, especially those whose sales depend heavily on weather or holiday influences. If the summer is abnormally hot, the producers of soft drinks, air conditioners, leisure-time equipment and related industries may naturally be expected to benefit. But if the summer is colder than usual, their earnings may be disappointing.

A cold, early winter would logically favor the heating equipment, oil and woolen goods industries, among others; while a long, open winter with an early spring would be a boon to the manufacturers of automobiles and parts, and lift the consumption of gasoline.

On the other hand, winter is a relatively poor season for the building industry, yet spring and fall are considered good periods for steel. Christmas and Easter bestow their calendar blessings on retail trade, while farm equipment makers anticipate spring and summer.

► Shop Early

What could be more natural than for stock market traders to try to take advantage of boom periods indicated by the calendar for these industries? By purchasing soft drink and air conditioning stocks in the summer; auto, auto parts, building and steel equities in the spring; dry goods issues shortly before Christmas and

Easter—in other words, at the onset of their busiest seasons—surely one should be able to reel in some profits.

However, the most logical course is not always the best to follow. Indeed, a person who buys hot weather stocks during the summer season may be disappointed to find that any prospective betterment has already been discounted, and the market climate for such stocks has veered suddenly in an opposite direction.

As Russell Sage used to advise: "Buy your straw hats in the winter." Hot weather items should be purchased in an off-season when *nobody* wants them, with the idea of selling at a time when *everybody* wants them.

▶ Unanimity of Opinion

A moment's reflection will show that important episodes in the market cannot possibly occur when the majority thinks they will. If, following a steep reaction, nearly everyone decides that the market will gradually decline further until the middle of April then, without a shadow of doubt, the bottom of the decline will come either earlier or later than the middle of April. Those who expect stocks to reach their lows in April will naturally sell their holdings sooner, with the intention of buying them back when they hit bottom. This selling in anticipation of bottom prices later on would probably be the cause of forcing stocks to their final lows much sooner than is generally expected. Moreover, if everybody believes that the top of the market will come in October, they will sell in August, or September, and then there would be no October top.

▶ Timing

One might assume, naturally enough, that when stocks open strong in the morning they might be expected to trend upward during most of the day. Then one could buy at the opening and sell later on at a profit. But it frequently happens that about 10:20 A.M., New York time, the market turns in the opposite direction from that in which it opened. This is because 20 or 30 minutes are required to dispose of the buy and sell orders that have accumulated overnight. Once they are out of the way, the market usually behaves according to whatever the latest business and international developments happen to be.

Likewise, around noon when men's energies are said to be highest and the market might be expected to be lofty too, there is a fair chance of having the lowest prices of the day, because of profit-taking from the West Coast, where there is a time differential, and because many floor traders go to lunch between 12 and 1 o'clock and are sometimes inclined to lighten positions beforehand.

▶ **Summer Solstice**

Many reasons might suggest a stiffening of stock prices in midsummer, when men spend more time in the open air and sunshine and, consequently, should have a more cheerful outlook and attitude toward life. But a study of the market for the years 1957-1961, inclusive, shows that if you purchased the 30 Dow-Jones Industrial stocks in early August and sold them late in October, you would have shown a loss 80 per cent of the time.

August, representing the peak of the vacation season, is a typically do-nothing month in the stock market: since 1900, the D-J Industrials reached their annual high once (1926) and their low only once (1921) during this month. This is probably because a man doesn't care to have to worry about stocks while he is on vacation, or to decide how the market will discount fall business prospects. Wishing to be relatively carefree while he is away, he may be inclined to close out his market position temporarily. Yet when he returns from vacation a month later, rested and optimistic, he may perhaps feel more confident about the future and buy back in again.*

* No one knows how much business is affected by the subtle influence of weather on human temperament. Dentists realize that patients are slow to make appointments and quick to break them on stormy days. A bad day depresses people and many may lack nerve to face the ordeal of having a tooth drilled. But the same thing that hurts

▶ *Up for the Holidays*

Under such circumstances one might naturally expect the stock market to branch upward. But statistics show that one can usually count on a slump in September, while November and December—stimulated as they are by the holidays and the year-end "dressing up" of institutional portfolios—are generally periods of rising prices. In this connection, it is interesting to see which months have experienced the most highs and lows in the past. At what time of the year are stock market bulls and bears the strongest?

DOW-JONES INDUSTRIAL AVERAGE

Annual Closing Highs Since 1900

Month		Year
January	11	1906, 1907, 1910, 1913, 1917, 1920, 1940, 1941, 1953, 1960, 1962
February	3	1903, 1931, 1934
March	4	1914, 1923, 1932, 1937
April	3	1902, 1930, 1956
May	1	1946
June	3	1901, 1911, 1948
July	4	1933, 1943, 1947, 1957
August	1	1926
September	4	1912, 1929, 1939, 1951
October	2	1918, 1922

the dentist's trade helps regular pill doctors. A lot of people whose spirits are dampened by the weather, or whose ills seem aggravated, think that if they visit a doctor and get a prescription from him, they will feel a great deal better.

Clients in most lines, however, bloom with the sunshine. Architects and real estate people find that comparatively few persons come in on a gloomy day to discuss new projects. A man owns a building lot, let us say, on the edge of town. On a rainy day his enthusiasm about the home he is thinking of building wanes somewhat. He decides to wait awhile.

DOW-JONES INDUSTRIAL AVERAGE

Annual Closing Highs Since 1900

November	9	1908, 1909, 1916, 1919, 1925, 1935, 1936, 1938, 1950
December	18	1900, 1904, 1905, 1915, 1921, 1924, 1927, 1928, 1942, 1944, 1945, 1949, 1952, 1954, 1955, 1958, 1959, 1961.

Annual Closing Lows Since 1900

Month		*Year*
January	13	1905, 1918, 1922, 1927, 1936, 1943, 1945, 1950, 1951, 1954, 1955, 1958, 1961
February	9	1908, 1909, 1912, 1915, 1919, 1928, 1933, 1944, 1959
March	6	1904, 1925, 1926, 1935, 1938, 1948
April	3	1916, 1939, 1942
May	3	1924, 1947, 1952
June	4	1913, 1940, 1949, 1962
July	4	1906, 1910, 1932, 1934
August	1	1921
September	3	1900, 1911, 1953
October	4	1923, 1946, 1957, 1960
November	5	1903, 1907, 1929, 1937, 1956
December	8	1901, 1902, 1914, 1917, 1920, 1930, 1931, 1941.

▶ Annual Sleigh Ride

Inspection reveals that annual highs on the Dow-Jones Industrials have been generally established after the summer months. Ascending in November, December and January, the Index reached its yearly peak during these months in 38 years out of 63 reviewed. Meanwhile, the bears' activity has been more evenly distributed. January, February and March account for 28 of the 63 lows; only a winter month claims more than five yearly bottoms. It seems that while the bulls, more often than not, like to kite stocks higher in the true spirit of Christmas, the bears are greasing the ways for a steep, wintry decline.

▶ Discounting in Advance

In today's market, the value and price of a stock are determined more by the company's average earnings trend over a period of months and years, rather than on snap judgments derived from a single twelve-months' showing, and much less from an isolated season. The seasons have some influence, to be sure, but it is far more customary now for the market to try to discount seasonal earnings variations by estimating results for the entire year and to compare June quarter profits, let us say, with the like period of a year ago, rather than the previous quarter.

▶ Seasonal Influences

Seasonal influences are no longer so meaningful to traders as they formerly were, yet such movements when they do occur are generally of three kinds:

Fluctuations caused by abnormal weather. Unusually high temperatures in the spring, or early summer, may spark a brief upturn in hot weather stocks, while a late, abnormally cold summer may trigger an opposite movement.*

Fluctuations scheduled by the calendar. When traders suddenly recall that this is the first day of summer, they may initiate purchases of hot weather issues, regardless of temperature. Also, the approach of Christmas, or Easter, will often spur up buying of retail company stocks.

Fluctuations based on prospective quarterly earnings variations. Generally speaking, this type of seasonal movement is the most reliable—provided, of course, that advance earnings estimates are well founded. However, buying should be done as far ahead as possible. As explained earlier, the market has a devilish penchant for discounting news or events well in advance and will often perform illogically, or contrary to what the majority expects, as soon as the motivating factors become public knowledge.

Seasonal movements of the first type are spasmodic, and those of the second are purely mechanical. One has to be unusually alert and agile to profit by them. While movements of the type sparked by quarterly earnings comparisons may provide many lucrative opportunities for traders, it is important to remember that the vast majority of stocks will have difficulty in pushing higher on improved earnings if the general market's prevailing trend happens to be down. (How many times, when the market is declining and bullish news published about a stock fails to stimulate much buying interest, have you said to yourself: "Why did they release such good news at a bad time like this?") Conversely, an unfavorable earnings report seldom upsets a stock so

---

* This same influence often affects retail trade. If there is a cold day early in September, people catch the notion of buying fall and winter clothing. Having started early to buy they generally keep it up. It is simply the same old story of one sheep jumping a fence and the others gaily following. Besides, one thing suggests another. The woman who acquires a handsome, expensive coat in September soon thinks of various things that she considers downright necessary to go with it. Last year's hat that she planned to do over will not do at all. And nothing could be more absurd than to wear a smart new coat and hat merely to cover a dress from last season. Thus it comes to pass that the friendly cold snap in September gives the merchant not only extra business right at the time, but extra business later on.

much when the over-all market is buoyant, as when the basic trend is downward.

▶ Bonanza Periods

Another peculiarity of seasonal activity is that in most stable years, stocks will normally experience at least two strong swings upward. This action stems fundamentally from the fact that around the first of January and July the owners of securities in this country receive huge sums in dividends and interest on their investments. Disbursements are made also in each quarter and sometimes every month. But at the beginning and middle of the year, the distributions are particularly heavy, and they tend to increase year by year in line with our national growth.

▶ Where the Money Goes

Most of this money goes to ordinary living expenses. Part of it pays old bills, or is channeled into travel and recreation. Some finds its way into real estate and other forms of investment. Yet many millions are used for buying securities. Thousands of private individuals, plus various funds, institutional investors, banks and insurance companies put this additional money into the market. This tends to make the demand for securities more active around the first of January and July than at any other time.

A comparison of the market from mid-December to mid-January, and from mid-June to mid-July, over a ten-year period, substantiates this phenomenon. Including 1960, when the trend of most stocks was consistently lower, and on three occasions when monthly price changes were virtually nil, the record shows that the Dow-Jones Industrials advanced from December into January and from June into July 75 per cent of the time. The midyear upswing and especially the year-end recovery, further stimulated as the latter is by extra dividend declarations and the end of the tax selling period, are cherished traditions in Wall Street.

But the trouble with traditional rallies or recoveries is that they either do not occur at all, or they have finished by the time the average person is ready to participate. Most of the upswing from the December 1961 low was accomplished in only a few days. When the Industrials ran into a wall of selling resistance between 735 and 740, they started a decline that carried to an intra-day low of 524.55 on June 25, 1962.

▶ Difference of Opinion

If the Spring Rise or the Year-End Rally arrives on schedule and the stocks one person holds participate vigorously, then that person will go around saying what a strong bull market it is. But another person holding stocks which reacted or remained dormant during the same period would undoubtedly claim it is a bear market. Both are right, of course.

▶ Perpetual Motion

Every trader naturally wants the market to move, for he can profit only when it does. The movements are important to him and are what he is continually looking for; hence his mental habits tend to become adjusted to the idea of perpetual motion. Even when the general market is standing still, independent fluctuations will be going on in both directions among individual stocks. This will create the illusion of motion, which the trader—in his desire for fast action—may misinterpret as applying to the whole market, and indicating the direction of the next intermediate trend.

When seasonal hopes are prevalent and a trader has fixed in his mind the wrong idea that the market must be always moving, he is at a disadvantage and is easily deceived. At the top of an advance, if the market is entering a quiet period while trying to consolidate its recent gains, a trader may not realize that the action is virtually stalemated. Seeing one stock spurt upward and then another, he is very likely to think that the whole market is still rising, when it may actually be standing still, or even drifting lower.

▶ **Dead Dog**

Conversely, at the tail end of a static period, the trader may say to himself in disgust: "This market is dead. Nothing doing now until the Spring Rise" . . . just as though the market had pledged itself to be perpetually active. Rather than studying the whole picture calmly and intelligently and trying to find out what background factors and future developments seem likely to haul the market from its rut, he lets faulty psychology get the upper hand and is easily taken over by cynicism and lethargy.

The market must go through occasional resting periods— just like human beings—when neither bullish, nor bearish, forces predominate. Until a new incentive appears, it will probably remain stationary, regardless of the weather, the seasons, and the hopes of impatient people. In such instances, the trader should act only after the new stimulus begins to assert itself. If he tries to anticipate it, he is only gambling, and in the end may find that, instead of *getting* Wall Street dollars, he is *furnishing* them.

▶ **Presidential Bugaboo**

Another of Wall Street's venerable legends that one must guard against concerns presidential elections. According to the theory—in season every four years—this represents a period when the only way that stocks can slant is upward, on the assertion that "a favorable economic and business atmosphere is essential around election time."

Admittedly there have been times in the past when election influences on business and the stock market were strong. In 1896, when William J. Bryan declared, "Thou shalt not crucify mankind upon this cross of gold," and free trade and free silver loomed on the economic horizon, stocks dropped like shot partridges.

Although the "Boy Orator" won the Democratic nomination, though not the Presidency, the market eroded further during the first year of the McKinley Administration.

The following table of market movements shows that the Dow-Jones Industrials closed higher in ten presidential years since 1900 and lower in six. While this may seem to confirm the idea that the market trends higher on average every four years, the over-all action in four of the ten quadrennial advancing periods was hardly convincing. For example, two decades of uninterrupted Republicanism ended in 1912 when Woodrow Wilson was elected over a split Republican ticket, yet the Industrials eked out only a slim 6.19 gain. In 1916, despite the economic and political significance of World War I, the average dipped 4.15 points; in 1948, the loss was a mere 3.86.

▶ Post-Election Years Negative

The post-election year record of eight advances offsetting eight declines refuses to substantiate any theories either. Indeed, the ebb and flow of stock prices today is not controlled by just one factor. History proves that business trends are increasingly impervious to political campaigns, that basic economic forces are stronger than politics.

The market can do anything, anytime—especially the unexpected—and to dogmatize, or depend exclusively on outside forces in forming conclusions about the securities price trend, or the business outlook, is merely to invite the penalty of serious error. Politics may exert a temporary dominating influence and again it may not. Yet many speculators are so tenacious in their beliefs and theories, that one may expect the bugaboos about Presidential Years, Spring Rises, Fall Setbacks, Indian Summer Declines and other phenomena to make their customary appearances until the end of time. They afford a fascinating theme of conversation, to be sure, yet they represent too often the foundlings of error which human frailties have placed on your doorstep.

An interesting sidelight to the Presidential Year Theory is

ANNUAL CLOSING PRICES D-J INDUSTRIALS

Pre-Election Year		Presidential Year		Change		Post-Election Year		Change	
1899	(66.08)	1900	(70.71)	Plus	4.63	1901	(64.56)	Minus	6.15
1903	(49.11)	1904	(69.61)	Plus	20.50	1905	(96.20)	Plus	26.59
1907	(58.75)	1908	(86.15)	Plus	27.40	1909	(99.05)	Plus	12.90
1911	(81.68)	1912	(87.87)	Plus	6.19	1913	(78.78)	Minus	9.09
1915	(99.15)	1916	(95.00)	Minus	4.15	1917	(74.38)	Minus	20.62
1919	(107.23)	1920	(71.95)	Minus	35.28	1921	(81.10)	Plus	9.15
1923	(95.52)	1924	(120.51)	Plus	24.99	1925	(156.66)	Plus	36.15
1927	(202.40)	1928	(300.00)	Plus	97.60	1929	(248.48)	Minus	51.52
1931	(77.90)	1932	(59.93)	Minus	17.97	1933	(99.90)	Plus	39.97
1935	(144.13)	1936	(179.90)	Plus	35.77	1937	(120.85)	Minus	59.05
1939	(150.24)	1940	(131.13)	Minus	19.11	1941	(110.96)	Minus	20.17
1943	(139.89)	1944	(152.32)	Plus	16.43	1945	(192.91)	Plus	40.59
1947	(181.16)	1948	(177.30)	Minus	3.86	1949	(200.13)	Plus	22.83
1951	(269.23)	1952	(291.90)	Plus	22.67	1953	(280.90)	Minus	11.00
1955	(488.40)	1956	(499.47)	Plus	11.07	1957	(435.69)	Minus	63.78
1959	(679.36)	1960	(615.89)	Minus	63.47	1961	(731.14)	Plus	115.25

this poem, written shortly after William Howard Taft of Yale made a presidential touchdown behind the interference of Harvard's Theodore Roosevelt. The direction of the market was unequivocally upward in 1908 and 1909, but Taft's victory apparently induced immediate profit-taking that didn't sit very well with the bulls. The moral of this: when Wall Street opinions are too unanimous—BEWARE!

'Twas the day before election and hope was in the air.
The Street was full of optimists and not a single bear;
The brokers in their offices were rushing to and fro,
With hardly time to take a breath, the orders poured in so.

Of Teddy's fate the Street was sure, and all with one accord
Agreed that at the polls he would be hustled overboard;
Then up and onward stocks would go, beyond their twelve-month high,
So everywhere was heard the cry of "Buy, O Broker, Buy!"

Alas! Alack! for human hopes! Though Roosevelt's schemes fell through,
From Wednesday's opening to the close the market heavier grew.
Those erstwhile bulls now cussed their luck and vowed to quit the game
And even yet they won't admit their judgment was to blame.

TOPICS:

- The theory that market prices tend to fluctuate with the seasons has won some credence in certain investment circles.

- Sales and earnings of certain industries obviously are affected by weather changes, but market prices may have discounted all this by the time the season arrives.

- Important episodes in the market cannot possibly occur when everybody thinks they will.

- The onset of winter and the Christmas season are generally bullish periods in the stock market.

- Since 1900, the Dow-Jones Industrials have posted their annual closing low more times in January than in any other month.

- Seasonal influences on the market are no longer so significant as they used to be; but such movements, when they do occur, are generally of three kinds.

- When general conditions are stable, the market normally experiences at least two strong swings upward during the year.

- The Presidential Year Theory holds that a presidential election is usually a bullish market influence, but a study of the market's action in the past 16 presidential years does not quite bear this out.

RULES:

1. It is a fallacy to depend too heavily on the occurrence of a Spring Rise, Indian Summer Setback, Year-End Recovery, etc.

2. August is the least decisive of any month in the stock market.

3. December is usually the most bullish month of the year.

4. The market tries to discount seasonal earnings variations by estimating corporate results for the entire year, and tends to compare quarterly profits with the like period of a year ago, rather than the previous quarter.

5. The demand for securities is usually very heavy in the early part of January and July.

6. When opinions in Wall Street are too unanimous— BEWARE! The market is famous for doing the unexpected.

The Remedy

Chapter 11

Fashions
in Formulas

December is a bad month to speculate in stocks. The others are April, July, November, May, August, March, January, September, June, October and February.
—Mark Twain

THE best way to keep people who should not speculate from doing so is to educate them as to its dangers. But no matter how often the dangers may be stressed, there are always certain people who just never will be convinced, except by their own personal experiences.

Many come to grief in their early struggles because they are obstinate and determined to rely on their own ingenuity. Unable to believe what others say about things that are hidden, they are tempted not just by curiosity, but by a love of excitement and especially the hope of gain. They see mergely the glittering surface of the market, and they rarely tell of their losses.

153

Losing is unpopular. It crushes pride and it wounds vanity. Somehow it always makes a person out to be rather a fool.*

Even those who lose consistently at speculation are nevertheless convinced that money can be made that way. If they had done this and that or the other, instead of what was done, of course the result would have been otherwise. They think that the failure of others to make a profit was caused by obvious mistakes that they themselves would naturally avoid.

But when confidence is finally jolted by a further string of losses—especially after the failure of one big coup that was intended to recover all—then some sort of system will be tried. By this time it is to be hoped that the bad judgment, which so far has prevented the speculator from understanding the necessity of machinery and a system, will not now prevent him from devising a plan and sticking to it. A train without a track is useless.†

To eliminate costly guesswork and remove discretion from situations where clear thinking may be swayed by too much optimism, or pessimism, many traders use mechanical timing or trading formulas, which prescribe definite action to take place when prices reach a certain level. By determining buying and selling points automatically, they reduce the responsibility of fund management to a simple application of the formula rules.

Formulas preclude selling at the top or buying at the bottom, except in rare instances. They contemplate action that is founded on the assumption that certain price levels will be attained eventually. If these levels have been touched before, the formula theorizes they will again. If they have never been reached, the formula assumes that they will.

* If a man buys a stock and it goes up in price, it is natural that he may go around telling everyone about his good judgment. But, should that stock collapse, instead of spiral, it is seldom ever mentioned. One reason is because the potential loss involved is with the individual too much already. He has no need to mention it to others. Whenever he studies the financial page, he thinks of it. His friends tease him about it—certainly his wife does. If he feels grumpy, or whiffs a golf shot, probably he was thinking too much again about IT!

† When you find, through experience in trading, that your losses are diminishing, you are actually gaining in a sense. Later, when you find that the gains more than offset the losses, then you are on the road to success. The difficulty is that too few people have enough fortitude to wait for that time to come. They just seem to lack the patience to try and *remake* themselves.

Formulas are essentially speculative. They do not and cannot guarantee against loss. But they represent an approach that can be very helpful to the person who is frustrated from trying to forecast market price trends and requires a definite plan of action.

▶ **The Fluid Portfolio**

The simplest type of formula divides the portfolio in two: common stocks constitute the aggressive side; bonds, preferred stocks and cash the defensive side. Exact proportions may vary according to individual requirements. But, since stocks are the volatile element, the plan is generally set in terms of a stock index that is geared to a "normal ratio" of prices over a period of time. Whenever the index reaches a predetermined level, above or below "normal," a certain percentage of stocks is switched automatically into bonds, or vice versa.

Take, for example, a portfolio that is half in common stocks and half in bonds. Normal is 600 on the Dow-Jones Industrials. A 10 per cent rise above 600 might call for a 10 per cent reduction in common stocks and a proportionate shift into bonds. A further advance of 10 per cent would reduce the common stock position to 30 per cent, while bonds are increased to 70 per cent. Reverse shifts occur from bonds into stocks during a declining period. Of course, if the market sold off sharply enough, or continued to move straight up, an all common stock, or a 100 per cent bond portfolio, would result.

The formula works best when the market's range of fluctuation is relatively narrow. When movements are wide, particularly at rising prices, results from the method are not so good. Obviously, no one would want to be all in bonds during an inflationary cycle, and the latter stages of a boom are generally the most explosive. Some accommodation should therefore be made for the possibility of prices pushing "through the roof."

▶ **Dollar Cost Averaging**

No formula in the world will prevent holdings from showing a loss when stocks drop below their original purchase prices. Yet by whittling the average of prices paid for stocks, it is possible to modify the risks which accompany any securities venture.

This may be accomplished by a formula process known as "dollar cost averaging," which lessens the frequency of loss and multiplies the occasions for profit. The formula requires that nearly identical amounts of money be invested at regularly spaced intervals of time, and it works best when stocks fluctuate widely.

Assume that an investor, who is able to save $100 a month, makes consecutive purchases of the same stock at 5, 4 and 2½ a share. The first month he buys 20 shares for $100, the second month 25 shares and the third month 40 shares. At the end of three months he has paid $300, excluding brokerage commissions, for 85 shares of stock. Average cost per share is approximately $3.83.

"Now wait a minute," somebody says. "Who in his right mind would persist in plunging more money into a low-priced stock that had already shed 50 per cent of its value in just eight weeks?"

That's true. But also consider the buyer's plight if he had invested his entire $300 when the stock was selling at 5. Average cost: $5, versus $3.83; number of shares acquired: 60, compared with 85.

Temporary price reactions are beneficial, in that you buy more shares when prices are low and fewer shares when they are high. Over the long run your purchases will have been made at a better-than-average price. That is the key to dollar averaging. Assuming that the stock you choose is not *always* in a declining trend, you will come out ahead.

The time interval between purchases is important, but not essential. So long as they are regularly maintained, purchases may be made monthly, quarterly, or even on a yearly basis. The amount to be employed is discretionary. But it should not be more than the investor is best able to set aside for use at a specific time. In their pamphlet "Personal Money Management," the American Bankers Association suggests the following savings schedules:

Monthly Income After Taxes	Monthly Savings
$1,000	$250-350
800	210-280
600	130-190
400	67-90
350	48-68
300	38-55
250	23-40
200	10-30

Dollar cost averaging appeals mostly to small investors, who wish to lay the cornerstone of a new portfolio, or add methodically to existing holdings. The plan is virtually the same as MIP (Monthly Investment Plan), sponsored by the New York Stock Exchange, which enables an investor to acquire stock on a regular, convenient basis, with payments as small as $40 every three months, or up to $1,000 a month.

▶ **The Stop Order**

Prudent trainmen and traders, who are aware of the dangers of rolling stock, always "Stop-Look-Listen" at critical crossings. By means of mechanical aids, they hope to preclude, or limit losses—thus assuring themselves of a clear track for intended future operations.

The "Stop" is a formula designed to protect paper profits in a lofty market, limit losses in a declining market, or initiate trades at crucial market levels. Sometimes known as the trader's "Mae West," it works best in a market which may be too high, but might bloom further upside.

Any order demanding an execution at a specified price whenever a round-lot sale of the same stock duplicates that price, is a Stop Order. If a trader buys 100 shares of U.S. Steel at 48 and wishes to limit his loss to about two points in the event of a reaction, he will enter an order to "Sell 100 Steel at 46, Stop." This means that whenever 100 shares of U.S. Steel sell at 46, the Stop will become effective automatically and the broker will try to execute at 46, the Stop price.

It is possible, however, that only 100 shares will sell at 46, and the next best bid is ¼ point, or more, below that level. Unless the original order set a specific limit of 46 ("Sell 100 Steel at 46, Stop Limit") the broker will offer 100 Steel for sale "at the market," with no guarantee of an execution at 46.

The same principle, applied to the buy side, is used to initiate trades already deemed advisable. Suppose a trader decides that General Motors is attractive after going through several weeks of sidewise price consolidation between 68 and 70. He has reason to believe that a strong upside breakout from this trading range is imminent that will carry the stock several points higher. But, not wishing to commit his funds until the expected move gets actually underway, he places an order to buy General Motors at 70¼ Stop GTC (Good 'Til Cancelled). He thus assures himself of participation in the advance, whenever a round-lot of General Motors changes hands at 70¼, or above.

Stop Orders provide round-the-clock protection and are used by most traders in some form. It is ridiculous to assert that half-point Stops are better than two, that three-point, or five-point Stops should always be used. Too much depends upon the trend of the market, the characteristics of the stock itself and the individual's requirements.

Addison Cammack, a broker from Kentucky, swore by the two-point Stop: "If you're wrong, you might as well be wrong for two points as ten." He followed this method successfully, and was one of the few bears to make a fortune in Wall Street and keep it.

Stop Orders should parallel the market the way Stop signs parallel the tracks. If the stock soars after entering a Stop, cancel and reenter the order at a price high enough to accommodate the scope and tempo of the rise. But set the price far enough below the prevailing level, so that only a serious drop, or a change in the market's trend, will touch it off.

Cancelling a Stop entirely, or lowering it as the stock nears a trading point, can be fatal in a fast sliding market. Born of hope that stocks will boom again, or fear of being "stopped out" at the bottom, this practice stems also from human weakness and snubs the very protection that Stops are supposed to provide.

It is natural when you buy a house to insure yourself immediately against fire loss; and protecting yourself with a Stop Order provides comparable insurance against a market loss. But, when used haphazardly by inexperienced persons, the Stop Order formula will differ from ordinary methods only in that it will require a slightly longer time for the gambler to lose his money. As the *Ticker* Magazine suggested in 1909:

> The fellow who fights and runs away
> Still lives to fight another day;
> Don't go in blind, quit trading rash.
> Use Stop-Loss Orders and save your cash.

▶ Scale Order Plan

Anyone buying a stock should automatically assume that it will probably dip below his original purchase price. If he catches the exact low, he should not confuse this good fortune with financial acumen. The trader who can recognize values and will agree with Jacob H. Schiff—"I never want to sell stocks near the top, nor buy them at the bottom"—should consider the merits of Scale Orders.

This method involves buying and selling additional shares of a stock at fixed intervals and to a prescribed point above or below the level of the initial commitment.

If a trader has a profit on 1,000 shares of stock in a market which he considers to be too high, but which might still advance some more, he may enter an order to sell his 1,000 shares on a ¼ point scale up from 50, let us say.

The operation will involve ten separate sell orders of 100 shares each, beginning with 50 and continuing at ¼ point intervals to 52¼. Conversely, the purchase of 1,000 shares on a similar scale would start at 50 and continue to 47¾. The principle is that, after the last 100 shares has been bought, a 50 per cent recovery of the decline from 50 would leave the trader long of 1,000 shares at 48⅞, without a loss. The price interval between purchases, or sales, and the point to which further commitments should be extended are problems for individual decision.

Scale Orders assist accumulation in a bull market, distribution in a top-heavy market and short selling in a bear market. The plan is helpful primarily to operators who know the approximate value of the stock in which they intend to deal. Buying additional shares or averaging down in a *poorly situated stock* is not intelligent speculation, but only gambling to satisfy vanity!

Usually it is safer to scale orders upward than downward. Many people who follow the method refuse to buy more of a stock until they can show a profit on their original purchase. After it has confirmed their belief that it would go up by actually doing so, this may be the time to get a little more. Another advantage of scaling on the way up—provided you keep within bounds—is that you are following the basic trend.

E. H. Harriman, the railroad magnate, once netted $58 million for the Union Pacific RR treasury by cleverly distributing huge bundles of Northern Pacific and Great Northern on a scale up. The same method helped George Breen unload $92 million worth of securities for a group of banks, without causing a ripple on the market. By scaling his purchases down, Benjamin Block, a commission broker, took on a 200,000 share line of U.S. Steel at an average price of 108 in 1927. Late the following year, he scaled the stock out again during a rise to 220.

These are not isolated examples. Indeed, success with the method is much too glowing. According to precedent, most stocks and the averages will retrace about half the distance between their high-low points and vice versa. In a sense, this is unfortunate, since power is claimed for the Scale Order system which it cannot hope to fulfill and causes it to be abused.

An actual test of the method would be too expensive, too impractical and would serve no useful purpose. There are few people today with enough fortitude, courage and patience for such an extensive, and what might be unsatisfying, campaign. Russell Sage used to say that Morgan, Carnegie and Rockefeller were the only men rich enough to really test the system ". . . and they had more sense."

The Scale Order is more fluid than the Stop, and it is a valuable addition to the "pistol pocket" of any trader. But it should only be used intelligently and in conjunction with other known market factors.

▶ *"Fill, or Kill"*

Many traders know the frustration of trying to get a report on the execution of a Limit Order, when the market is boiling on a late tape. By the time "nothing done, stock ahead," or "matched and lost" is flashed back from the trading floor, the stock may have galloped anywhere from a large fraction to a point or more.

The only way to guarantee an execution is via a Market Order. But, because this can be costly sometimes, especially with a thin market and fast-moving issues, traders often rely on an Immediate Order when dealing in round-lots.

The Immediate Order, also known as "Fill, or Kill," demands a prompt execution at a stipulated price. If it cannot be filled at that price, the order is "killed" automatically and a fresh quote is supplied from the trading floor. Instead of delay and uncertainty you know instantly where you stand. This will enable you to re-enter the order at a new price limit, or place a Market Order to buy at the best price obtainable.

Immediate Orders demand fast action. Applying to both sides of the market, they can also be used for selling short, provided they meet the requirements of the short selling rule. They are particularly effective in a busy market when the ticker is running late and telephone system quotes are often unreliable. Izaak Waltons of finance should consider using this device when angling in the troubled waters of the market place.

These five operating methods are favored by those who believe in a systematic approach to the stock market. But the one method in which more people seem to have blind faith than any other is the chart. Charts have many advantages. They are scholarly in appearance and quite easy to read. However, as discussed in the next chapter, they also have certain shortcomings; they are useful as an aid to speculation, but they are by no means infallible.

▶ Dr. Jekyll and Mr. Hyde

The question now arises: "Can a man be *told* how to speculate in the market?" Of course, he can *learn* how to speculate, and the means of learning have been described frequently in print. But speculation also demands careful training. Who would dare to claim proficiency in law or engineering without the necessary practice and experience that books cannot provide?

If two men of the same age and intelligence started to work simultaneously in the same company at adjacent desks, studying the same rules and principles of the business, and making similar observations and experiencing comparable things, it would be natural to suppose that their relative achievements after a certain time would be almost identical. But this would not necessarily hold true: for one reason, because of their physical and temperamental differences; for another, because of the diverse ways in which they applied themselves. The man who was conscientious, with the most will power, perseverance and the best work habits, would undoubtedly be the winner and have the greatest chance of becoming the top banana of that whole office bunch.

Many men have had 25 years or more experience operating in the stock market, either as investors or speculators. They have run the gamut of cyclical booms and busts. They can peel off accurate facts and figures relating to all kinds of stocks and bonds.

Yet they often are not so successful as other men, who know less about the mechanics and background of the market but have learned to apply themselves honestly, diligently and enthusiastically—day after day and month after month—in exploring the basic psychological, statistical and technical influences that stimulate stock price movements.

As mathematicians are adept at figures and musicians are clever with notes, so is it important that you try to understand yourself and others better, and thus attain perfection in your ability to play upon the greatest of all instruments, the human mind.

▶ Room at the Top

The main point is that knowledge about yourself will help you to analyze your weak points and convert them into strong ones. If you neither recognize nor try to conquer them, they will simply remain with you, continually undermining your chances. Everyone has a door to his innermost thoughts; a gateway, indeed, to his entire life. The gateway is bolted and secured by a chain, held fast by a padlock. But there is a key to the padlock and the man who has it and can turn it easily will succeed where others fail. This applies to politics, industry, sports, diplomacy, the stock market, and any other endeavor.

▶ Lady Luck

One of the first ideas a trader must learn to discard is that success in speculation depends entirely upon luck. Some luck is involved in most ventures, to be sure, and when one trade turns out better than another, a person may say to himself: "That was lucky." Yet the fact is that the elements which caused it to turn out so well were already present—only he didn't see them. Just as when failure comes, the element of failure was already there. The loss on the trade should not be ascribed entirely to bad luck.

Another mental hazard to guard against is blind faith in

the suggestions of other men. Of course, the novice in any field must lean on a wiser person until he assimilates some aspects of the business and tries, perhaps, to improve upon it for his own use. But when you see a man who has been successful in the market, remember that you are looking at the finished product. You don't know and may never know the detours and the difficulties he had to get there. No cosmonaut could ever cope with all the demands put upon him in outer space if he had not been thoroughly prepared beforehand. By applying the knowledge gained from analyzing your past mistakes, perhaps you too can soar to heights far above what you previously would have considered possible.

▶ No Perfect Formula

Remember that no formula or system is so perfect that it cannot be improved upon. This applies certainly in the stock market. Too much trust in a method or a system is a bad thing; any formula plan must be paired with sound judgment coming from a mature mind. Yet it is also trite to say that all systems are worthless, or that a person who follows them will eventually be living on just pauper pills.

Most mechanical timing, or trading, formulas have been quite thoroughly studied and none has been found perfect. One reason is because imperfect human beings are involved. But that is no reason to join in the clamor against them. The greatest opponents of any system generally reveal that their own principal weak spot has been the mental block that made them susceptible only to the weakness of the system itself. Eliminate trust in any system you do not understand, but still believe in the basic idea of the system.

All stock market formulas at least contain a more or less workable idea and, to be successful at trading, you must find out how these ideas can be best applied. Like produces like and if your idea is good, it will produce good. A man's character and mental attitude, the way he educates himself, and the method or system he uses to develop his self-mastery are the principal determinants of whether he wins or loses. In the long run, you will find that thinking your own thoughts is much easier and more profitable than trying to guess what is on the other fellow's mind.

TOPICS:

- No matter how often the dangers of speculation are stressed, some people will never be convinced except by their own experience.

- Many traders follow mechanical formulas designed to eliminate guesswork and remove discretion from situations where clear thinking may be swayed by too much optimism or pessimism.

- The simplest type of formula divides the portfolio in two: bonds, preferred stocks and cash, versus common stocks.

- Dollar Cost Averaging.

- The Stop Order.

- The Scale Order Plan.

- The Immediate Order.

- A man can be *told* how to speculate, but can he *learn* how to speculate?

- The part played by luck in market operations.

- All stock market formulas at least contain an idea, and you must find out how those ideas can be best applied.

RULES:

1. Mechanical timing or trading formulas preclude selling at the top or buying at the bottom, except in rare instances.

2. Dollar cost averaging works best with stocks that fluctuate widely. If the stock you choose is not *always* in a declining trend, you should come out ahead.

3. Stop Orders work best in a market which may be too high, but might carry further.

4. Never cancel a Stop, or lower it, as the stock nears a trading point in a fast sliding market.

5. Success with a Scale Order depends largely on knowing the approximate value of the stock in which you intend to deal.

6. Immediate Orders are useful for removing delay and uncertainty and knowing instantly where you stand in the market.

7. Try to analyze your weak points and convert them into strong ones.

8. Forget the idea that speculation depends entirely upon luck, and guard against blind faith in the suggestions of other men.

9. No formula or system is so perfect that it can't be improved upon.

10. Eliminate trust in any system you do not understand, but still believe in the basic idea of the system.

Chapter 12

Caution:
Chart Line
Crossing

MANY clever operators trade in the market by means of charts, which show the price movements of a stock day by day, or even hourly, over a period of many months, together with the volume of sales and their relation to price fluctuations. A study of such charts often helps to determine the accumulation (buying) levels and the distribution (selling) levels of certain stocks.

The chart of Technicolor, Inc., prior to its sensational upward thrust early in 1961, would have shown to an observer that the stock had several times sold above 9 and then sunk back to the 6-7 level without ever going below that mark.

► Mousetrap

According to the technical price pattern, Technicolor should have been bought anywhere below 10, and a person who so bought it could have quadrupled his money within a year. But other stocks indicating strong support levels only excite a person into buying something that may soon decline in price. A certain chemical stock recently had a habit of fluctuating in the low 70's for several weeks. Whenever it dipped to 71, it seemed to lose interest in going much lower. Many bought the stock because of the way it looked on the chart. Then came a time when it never stopped going down until it carried close to 50. Later it sagged some more. By that time many who had bought in the 70's became alarmed and sold at a substantial loss. In other words, it is easier to keep a chart than to interpret its story. Even experienced chart readers confess that it sometimes is difficult to distinguish between accumulation and distribution.

► Draw Play

A chart is simply a piece of graph paper on which is recorded each day as they occur, the price changes that have taken place in a particular stock, a group of stocks, or the general market, with attendant trading volume.

There is no hocus pocus, or deep mystery, connected with charting. The posting or recording of prices is purely mechanical. But to assume, as many seem to do, that the riddle of market movements may be solved by filling in some lines on graph paper every day is buncombe. If the system were foolproof, it would have been discovered and made public property long ago. This would have nullified its usefulness automatically. If everybody kept charts and knew exactly when to buy and sell, to whom would they sell to at the top, or buy from at the bottom? Every transaction demands both a buyer and a seller. One party is doing the right thing at the right time and the other is doing the wrong thing at the same time.

▶ *Admit Mistakes*

When relied upon as a system for beating the market, charts have little value; but when used as an *aid* to intelligent speculation, or investment, they can be very helpful.

Any serious student of the technical approach spends many hours each day weighing the pros and cons of his work. He understands that charts have certain shortcomings. He realizes that a price trend may be already underway before a buy or sell signal shows clearly on the chart. He knows also that stocks do not necessarily move together, even with other issues in the same group, any more than brothers and sisters in a large family can be expected to perform similarly.

On the other hand, the untrained person who spends about 10-15 minutes daily working on charts cannot really be called a chartist. He bases his buying or selling action too much on snap interpretations of what the chart "says." Rather than admit an error and change course if his "reading" goes awry in the early stages, he glues himself stubbornly to the stock, always hoping for a rally to release him from his self-sewn strait jacket.

▶ *Past Records*

It is a great mistake to presume that the future is a repetition of the past, but it is as much a fallacy to suppose that charts cannot help to calculate the future.

Charts cannot forecast unpredictable happenings such as wars, or acts of God, which have a profound influence on market movements. Sudden events, like "Ike's" illness in 1955, or Russia's launching of Sputnik I in 1957, will also confuse the technician. But, provided that false breakouts and the inevitable errors of interpretation are guarded against, charts are a generally reliable guide to lean upon.

Nearly all businessmen consult past records when trying to plan ahead. Their judgment of the future is influenced by what such data show. If you study a person's record and the past has been good, you are likely to judge favorably about his future. Likewise, a photograph will help you to recognize a man and his qualities better than merely a brief description of him. You may be able to retain in your mind the past movements of stocks in which you are interested. But why burden the mind with abstract quotations, when they can be pictured? A graphic description will get over the idea of what a stock is like more clearly than the same thought could ever be conveyed in words.

▶ Pass, or Punt

There are four principal methods of operating in the market: buy, sell, sell short, or hold. When trying to decide which to follow, of course, it is important to consult other aids besides charts. If a stock appears cheap on the basis of higher projected earnings and a strong chart pattern it may be a candidate for purchase. But, statisticians and technicians can only assume a stock's value. The sole factor in determining its *actual* value is public opinion. The market has proved this countless times. An experienced chartist and a trained statistician working together represent about as formidable a team as can be found in Wall Street—but they must continually recognize the importance of keeping their most sensitive finger on the public's pulse.

▶ The Confidence Factor

Many stocks are often underpriced on a fundamental basis, just as others are frequently overpriced. In the spring of 1962, panic-type liquidation toppled the Dow-Jones Industrials about 25 per cent from their March peak and culminated in a 14¾ million share climax trading session on May 29, with the ticker running more than two hours behind actual floor transactions. Business was favorable at the time and corporate reports for the first quarter generally were very good. From a statistical, or fundamental, viewpoint, selected purchases seemed warranted. But, investor confidence was deteriorating commensurately with the drop in security values, and when the technical market pattern began to flash warnings of an impending storm, many professional chartists used this as a reason to take cover.

▶ Double Reverse

Contrary to popular belief, the trends of business and the market often move in opposite directions. In 1946, the business trend was up, but stock prices collapsed and the same thing happened in the January-June period of 1962. On the other hand, while earnings declined early in 1949, stocks were buoyant.* About 75 per cent of market movements are caused by changing technical and fundamental conditions, and 25 per cent stem from shifts in public sentiment. Of these, the latter has been and will always be the most difficult and frustrating to correctly analyze and forecast.

▶ Other Teams in the League

In the summer of 1959, after distribution in the machinery group had been accomplished, the prices of these stocks naturally began to wilt. They reached even lower levels in the fall of 1960. But, when speculative sentiment perked up again the following January, many individuals bought heavily. They were easily encouraged into buying because they remembered the rise these stocks experienced from 1953 to 1957 and from February 1958 to July 1959. Everybody figured that since the group had helped pace a rise on two previous occasions, it naturally followed that it would be one of the forerunners of the next bull upmove. Such reasoning!

A comparable situation prevailed in the coppers, which reached a top in 1956 and the steel and farm equipment groups when they posted peaks in 1959. While the coppers thudded lower in 1957 and the steel, farm equipment and machinery issues fell in 1960, everybody said: "Buy the steel, farm equipment and

---

* The market's contrariness can be further illustrated by the fact that when World War II began, the D-J Industrials advanced 23 per cent, but when the Korean War broke out the average dropped 14 per cent. In January-June 1949, when steel-labor negotiations were underway, the market went up; but early in 1962, when steel was again a dominant factor, the market went into a steep decline.

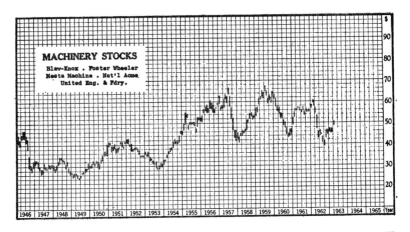

MACHINERY STOCKS
Blaw-Knox . Foster Wheeler
Mesta Machine . Nat'l Acme
United Eng. & Fdry.

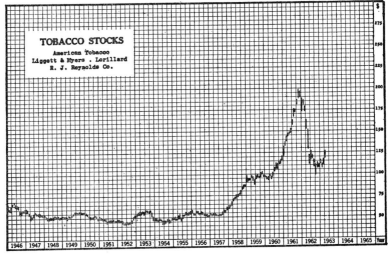

TOBACCO STOCKS
American Tobacco
Liggett & Myers . Lorillard
R. J. Reynolds Co.

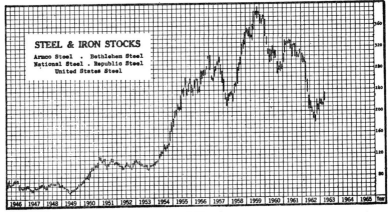

STEEL & IRON STOCKS
Armco Steel . Bethlehem Steel
National Steel . Republic Steel
United States Steel

172

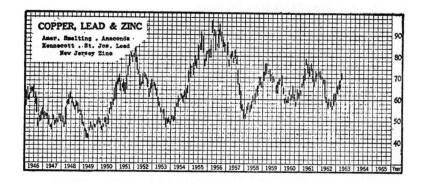

COPPER, LEAD & ZINC
Amer. Smelting . Anaconda .
Kennecott .. St. Jos. Lead
New Jersey Zinc

| 1946 | 1947 | 1948 | 1949 | 1950 | 1951 | 1952 | 1953 | 1954 | 1955 | 1956 | 1957 | 1958 | 1959 | 1960 | 1961 | 1962 | 1963 | 1964 | 1965 | Year |

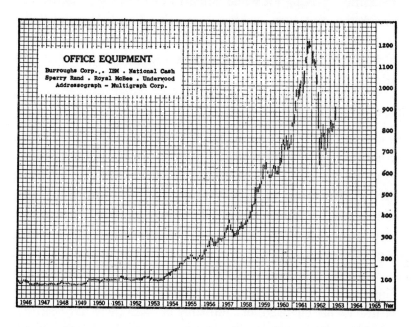

OFFICE EQUIPMENT
Burroughs Corp... IBM . National Cash
Sperry Rand . Royal McBee . Underwood
Addressograph - Multigraph Corp.

| 1946 | 1947 | 1948 | 1949 | 1950 | 1951 | 1952 | 1953 | 1954 | 1955 | 1956 | 1957 | 1958 | 1959 | 1960 | 1961 | 1962 | 1963 | 1964 | 1965 | Year |

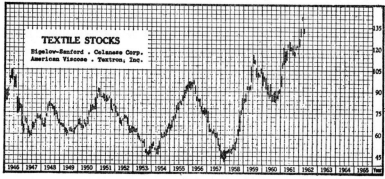

TEXTILE STOCKS
Bigelow-Sanford . Celanese Corp.
American Viscose . Textron, Inc.

| 1946 | 1947 | 1948 | 1949 | 1950 | 1951 | 1952 | 1953 | 1954 | 1955 | 1956 | 1957 | 1958 | 1959 | 1960 | 1961 | 1962 | 1963 | 1964 | 1965 | Year |

173

copper stocks. Among the safest buys in the world. Leave textile, tobacco, insurance and office equipment stocks alone. Too speculative. Just look what happened to textiles in 1956 and 1957." And much more similar humbug.

▶ **Shifts in the Line-up**

If it should be noted that five commuters a day slip and fall in a station parking lot while going to or from their trains during the winter, and then suddenly one day twenty persons fall, it would not mean that commuters were becoming more unsteady on their feet. Probably more ice and snow had accumulated in the parking lot.

Likewise, a newsstand proprietor has 150 Sunday papers, let us say, but can only sell one hundred of them. So the following Sunday he orders only a hundred papers. And on that day perhaps he could have sold a far greater number. In his opinion, humans are much too erratic about their Sabbath-day reading habits and it is hopeless trying to predict what they will want. But chances are that on the Sunday when the demand for papers was so great, there was bad weather to keep more people indoors, or something of greater interest was in the paper than the weekend previous.

As applied to the stock market, if the average trader does one thing today and something else next week, it is not necessarily because he has changed, but probably because there has been some shift in conditions.

With a record of past performances and current influences, it should be easier to tell in advance about an average man than an average stock. For one thing, since there are more men than stocks, it is possible to get the average a little closer. To know all the factors that prompt an individual investor to act thus and so is practically impossible, but when we consider the entire investing public, the task is much less difficult. And the larger the investing public, the easier it is to predict what the average person is likely to do.

▶ **Insuring the Players**

Insurance companies know with uncanny accuracy the average man's chances for a long life. They know that under certain conditions—age, climate, occupation and so on—so many men will be careless and set fire to their homes. A certain number will run into guileless pedestrians with high-powered automobiles and be sued for damages. And a known number of cars out of every thousand will be stolen each year.

The company does not place its faith in the man who takes out insurance, no matter how well mannered, intelligent, or wealthy he appears. It does not say that Mr. Blank is much too refined and careful to burn down his house, or drive over somebody, or fail to remove his key from the ignition in a crowded city. The company knows that a certain number of men are going to do these very things every year. What it doesn't know is who the men are and how, or when, they will do them. In other words, the company simply considers such variations from normal behavior as being unpredictable, which of course they are.

In the same vein, a chartist's decision to buy or sell is based partly upon his conclusions drawn from studying a certain stock's record of behavior in the past. He realizes that there have been and will in future be occasional variations. But his experience tells him that such abnormalities usually prove to be temporary. When stocks get too high in price, or too low—these are variations from normal. No one can forecast exactly when or why or in what stocks the abnormalities will occur. Yet when they actually take place, or seem on the verge of doing so, the alert chartist will be prepared and waiting with an order pad.

▶ **Quarterback of the Market**

Another important factor to sift for clues to market movements is the daily share volume. Because it measures buying and selling pressure, the turnover is closely related to security price changes.

Thus, when a single stock or the market moves over a relatively wide range, it means that purchases or sales are being carried out in quantity. Also important to know is the capitalization (number of shares outstanding) of the stock being observed. A heavily capitalized stock will naturally require more action to make it move significantly than will a stock whose capitalization is smaller. When aligned with the volume of actual transactions, this information indicates what percentage of total shares outstanding is being traded to influence the move. Like the quarterback on a football team, volume calls the signals for the next phase of action.

Volume is always heaviest in a falling market. In August 1857, when transactions topped 70,000 for a day, panic was in the saddle. Three million shares were traded initially under similar conditions in 1901; while liquidation in December 1916 produced a like amount for the second time. Dwindling thereafter until November 10, 1925, which saw 3,390,900 shares traded, the volume picked up in the late 1920's, touching an all-time peak of 16.4 million during the 1929 debacle.

▶ Goal Line Stand

In addition to high volume days, the sessions of low turnover are significant. Memorable in this respect were the 15,800 shares exchanged by 32 frosty brokers during the Blizzard of 1888. The slowest day since 1900 was December 30, 1914, when 49,937 shares changed hands. In the 1920's, trading ebbed to a meager 226,748 shares on June 29, 1920. In the 1930's, the dullest session was July 3, 1939, with 235,140 shares, while August 19, 1940, got the palm for that decade with a stingy 129,650.

Accustomed as we may be to high speed tickers, electric quotation boards and a daily turnover of about 3-4 million shares, it is difficult to understand how brokers a century ago seemed satisfied in transacting only eight or nine thousand shares a day. But just as their 1963 counterparts thankfully recall that no day's volume dipped below the half-million level in fifteen years, so too undoubtedly did brokers in 1860 look back three decades to March 16, when the total dribbled to an all-time, 31-share low. On that bleak occasion, anyone with $3,470.25 could have controlled business for the entire session: five shares of Morris Canal & Banking Co. and 26 shares of U.S. Bank.

▶ The Scoreboard

Although standards have altered over the years, the significance of volume versus price change remains unchanged. Some professionals claim that forecasting a decline by volume studies is easier than interpreting an advance. While this is possible, it is equally certain that no large amount of stock can be accumulated, or distributed, without the turnover expanding commensurately. Buyers must be more aggressive than sellers, or vice versa, and a relatively large percentage of the stock outstanding must be traded for the market to move significantly up or down, unless the market for the stock involved is unusually thin.

When volume varies markedly from the normal daily average, it may be signaling an important move. For this reason, attention should be alerted for increased activity, especially if it occurs around an area where resistance or support materialized before.

Although the signal it gives is sometimes false, or premature, volume is a good barometer of the market. As such, it considers day-to-day transactions to be meaningless, except insofar as they fit into the over-all pattern contributing to a breakout from an established trading range.

▶ Team Mascot

A person must guard against becoming sentimentally attached to a stock. Market pets are luxuries that most people can ill afford. It is an axiom of human nature to favor a stock that has treated you well in the past, or a behind-the-market issue that seems certain to blossom. Perhaps it was recommended by a dear friend of your mother's who told you to "Buy it and put it away!" It is almost sad to hear a person describing such and such a stock in Technicolor terms, trying to endow his pet with all kinds of virtues, while any unbiased individual can see that it has little to distinguish it from dozens of other issues. Every stock must be *someone's* pet and the reasons for favoring it are usually just about alike.

One hears a trader extolling, for instance, the merits of a stock which he claims will protect it from going down much even in the event of a general market slide. The stock pays good dividends, the sales-earnings trend and order backlog are up, finances of the company are strong and its young and aggressive management team is very research-minded. Because the technical pattern looks bullish too, the stock is certain to stand firm even if the rest of the market should collapse. HUMBUG—IN EXCELSIS! When the hen house is raided *all* the chicks go.

▶ Your Nemesis

Just as it is unwise ever to put a halo around a stock, so should a trader recognize that there are always certain issues that never seem to make money for him. The two of them are real poison together. The trader invariably gets aboard too soon, or disembarks too late. Whether he goes long of the stock or sells it short, the operation somehow ends in a loss.

Nothing merely happens in the market and there are psychological demons responsible for this. Among them are stubbornness and hope. Therefore, when you meet up with a stock that refuses to be friendly—*leave it alone*. Repeat to yourself these words: "Don't—Do Not—Do It Not!" There is no room in the market place for generosity or sentiment.

▶ Offensive-Defensive Action

Stocks may be aggressive and positive, providing much of the leadership, or defensive, dull and uninteresting. It is almost as easy to forecast the way a stock will perform by knowing it and watching and studying its traits and habits over a period of time as it is to forecast what a certain person may do after you have known him for a while.

It is an old saying that all stocks need a sponsor, a "daddy," to bolster them and this is possibly true. With about 1,100 different issues listed on the New York Stock Exchange alone, why should anybody pick out one stock rather than another, unless that stock has gathered a market following and established a reputation? In other words, why should anybody pick out an unadvertised stock that rarely fluctuates much and seldom appears on the ticker tape, any more than one should buy an unadvertised tooth paste rather than a brand that everybody is talking about? The real power which forces higher prices is the buying by thousands of small investors and small speculators. You and I, and all the rest like us, are the ones who really put prices up. Without us the market would be dull indeed.

▶ **Learn the Signals**

Before investing or trading in a stock, you should look into its statistical history. Note where previous support and resistance levels are located by studying its chart. Here are a few of the questions that many professional technicians ask themselves about a stock: Does it tend to make flat, round, or spike tops? Has it sold off sharply from head and shoulders formations in the past? How does it perform after making a breakaway gap, and how many double and triple top or bottom patterns does its chart picture show? Does it have any special tendency to form wedges, islands, flags, saucers, diamonds, or rectangles? What about ascending or descending triangles?

Market prices are made by people. Consequently, they reflect the thoughts of the mind and reveal the massed hopes, fears, actions and desires of human beings. If used as a blind guide for speculation, charts can lead to ruin. But they can be invaluable when used intelligently by a person attempting to project the foreseeable future from the demonstrated past.

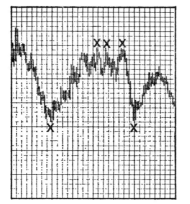

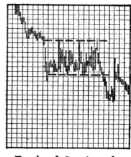

Typical Rectangle
Formation

Double Bottom
and Triple Top

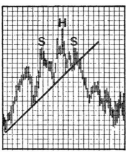

Head and Shoulders

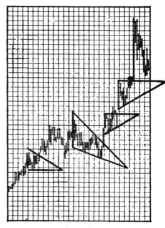

Triangles

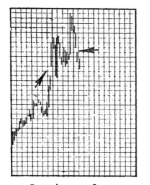

Breakaway Gaps

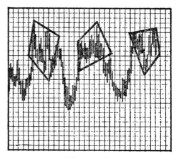

Diamonds

Spike Tops

Flags

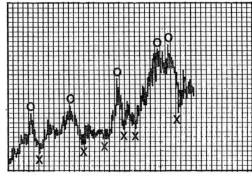

**A Series of Ascending Upside Resistance
(0) and Downside Support (X̄) Levels**

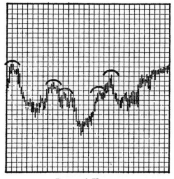

Round Tops

Islands (lower left)

TOPICS:

• Many clever operators trade in the market by means of charts; but it often is difficult to distinguish between accumulation and distribution.

• Charts are helpful for calculating the market's future.

• Four principal methods of operating in the market.

• Stock market and business trends often move in opposite directions.

• The daily share volume is a helpful clue to market price movements.

• Market pets are expensive luxuries.

• Everybody has a stock, or stocks, he never seems to make money in.

• Market prices are made by people.

• What are some of the questions a professional chartist asks himself about a stock?

RULES:

1. Every transaction demands both a buyer and a seller.

2. Charts are useless as a system for beating the market.

3. You should consult other market aids besides charts.

4. The real factor in determining a stock's actual value is public opinion.

5. About 75 per cent of market movements are caused by fundamental and technical conditions, and 25 per cent by psychological changes.

6. Volume is always heaviest in a falling market.

7. Never be sentimental about a stock.

8. There is no room in the market place for generosity or sentiment.

9. Stocks often need a sponsor to bolster them.

10. Before investing in a stock, look into its history.

Chapter 13

Turns With
a Tape Worm

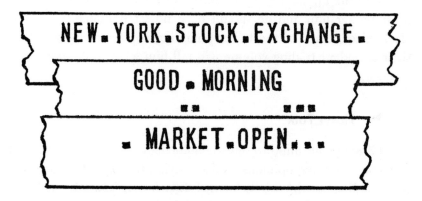

NEW.YORK.STOCK.EXCHANGE.

GOOD.MORNING

.MARKET.OPEN...

TAPE reading is a form of scientific speculation based on experience which enables a trader to determine how stocks will perform over the near-term. By studying the hieroglyphics changing constantly on a narrow band of paper called "ticker tape," skilled traders can decide what to buy for a rise, what to sell short for a fall and what to avoid altogether. Like the Oracle of Apollo at Delphi, the tape never lies. It merely presents the facts for the reader to interpret.

A person who studies stocks and knows their symbols as tickers have been printing them since November 1867, when the first machine appeared in Wall Street, obviously can read the tape. But reading the tape to find out the prevailing trend of the market, or certain last sales is one thing; and reading the tape to weigh the trading outlook for different stocks is quite another.

An actor must have special talents to become a star. Talent plus hard work may make him a genius. The same holds true of tape reading. But a Master's Degree can be acquired only by close observation and experience, and a long and tedious apprenticeship.

First of all, the tape reader must have the talent of his profession. A broad, fundamental understanding of the market is necessary. He should study price movements day by day, making notes and records, until it becomes natural for him to digest and analyze the story the tape is telling without their help. No external forces must bother him and he should have no set opinions. Only the clack, clack, clack of the ticker pounding out price changes with their attendant trading volume will tell him what to do and when to do it.

▶ Ticker Talk

Closing your mind to outside influences is not at all easy. You can't help forming opinions while studying the tape. If your stock takes a dive, or the whole market tilts lower, you may subconsciously say to yourself: "They don't look good to me," or "The rails should be sold," or "The steels act toppy." Human nature always compels you to reach some conclusion. The electric quotation board kind of digs at you too. The noise it makes when racking up price changes sounds too much like a snicker if you are losing money.

Everything one sees, or hears, or feels, or smells in the electrified atmosphere of a board room impresses the mind in some form. It is humanly impossible to gaze at the tape and listen to all the rumors and gossip floating around without becoming biased in some way.

Rather than holding a stock you bought after careful study and waiting patiently for it to reach your expected price, the board room lingo and the generally uninformed opinions of other people will probably make you kick it overboard the first time the market takes a dip, when perhaps you should be buying more.

▶ Hot Air

A common expression heard around the ticker is "I wouldn't buy that 'dog' with wooden money!" Yet a careful study of the situation and the tape action of the stock might show it to be a most attractive purchase.

It is loony the way some people pile in or out of stocks just on another's say-so. One trader will ask a friend: "What do you think of Standard?" The answer will be: "I don't like it."

The same question addressed to a third party will prompt a reply: "It should be sold"; so the trader sells some short, merely because two men's opinions confirmed each other. Three people thus have had a hand in initiating a transaction without any of them even pausing to look the stock up. If Standard is selling at 40 and 500 shares are sold, the transaction would involve $20,000. What a lot of money to bet on just hot air!

▶ Tranquilizers, Anyone?

One of the nervous habits peculiar to board rooms is that no matter how slow or dull the market may be, all eyes will be riveted on the tape. Sometimes a watcher will get up and pace the floor, berate the market for being so inactive, complain to the next fellow that there is absolutely no trend at all, and then plunk himself moodily in the same chair again and gape at the tape for another hour. This habit becomes so ingrained sometimes that men have been known to glare at symbols and prices even after the market is shuttered for the day and only the bid-and-asked quotations are being run off. Some people seem to believe that the act of thinking is closely associated with the act of watching the tape; but as George Gershwin said to the piano, "It Ain't Necessarily So."

Conditions shift so rapidly in the market that untrained tape watchers find it impossible to tell whether a basic change is taking place, or if the move is only temporary and the main trend remains intact. The average trader tends to consider only the last sales bobbing in front of him. He seldom looks ahead. His actions are geared to short-term movements, and are based mostly on news and views in the morning paper, corporate statistics just recently published, or some scrap of information he has heard.

▶ **Fact and Fancy**

The more statistics, opinions, reports, résumés and other printed material a trader reads, the farther is he removed from the market's present state. He may not realize that the vast majority of such data has been discounted, and the profits or losses derived therefrom have long since been printed on tape that is already curled in the ticker basket.

Statistics and news are to the market what thunder is to lightning. Genuine news is unexpected—like lightning in a cloudless sky. Statistics are valuable, but they are sometimes too old.

It usually is wiser to act on general information than on special information, which may be misleading. General information includes over-all economic and business conditions, the cold war situation—anything that is viewed in a broad perspective.

Statistics are usually subordinate to the panoramic view. Those who confine themselves too closely to statistics or, especially, to them alone, are poor advisers. It has been correctly said that "Nothing is so fallacious as facts, except figures." It is true also that no grist can be ground with water that has already run past the mill. For these reasons it is necessary to differentiate between what has been, what is now and what the future may be in planning any investment or trading program.

PAST	PRESENT	FUTURE
Financial articles and corporate releases appearing in daily newspapers; most market reports, reviews, résumés, etc. Generally speaking, all published statements. Anything that is already an *established fact*.		Growth projections based on probable future earnings trends; sales estimates derived from official sources and firm orders on the books; technical and fundamental factors, which indicate business and stock market conditions 3-6 months hence.

▶ What Happened?

Market movements are generally surprises, or disappointments. As a matter of fact, most short-term fluctuations are unlooked for, unexpected and unanticipated. When an advance seems most probable a decline may be imminent; when a reaction is expected a rise may occur. Not even "Mary, Mary" of nursery rhyme fame is quite so contrary as the stock market has often proved itself to be.

To win consistently at tape reading, a man must have special mental equipment, a natural aptitude for speculation and an awareness of how human emotions will try to sway his thoughts and actions when stock prices change radically. Some influential traders have a private ticker at home, or in the office, so they can formulate their opinions more on what they see and know and less on what they hear. Most men important enough to be in big league affairs cannot possibly spare more than a few moments once or twice a year in their broker's office. They seem to follow the thesis that "the bee that gets the honey doesn't hang around the hive."

▶ The Ticker Bug

Only the most experienced and talented traders should hang around the ticker, lest they be tempted to overtrade. Traders who are mostly interested in catching intermediate swings may derive some benefit from daily tape gazing. But investors who make portfolio changes only a few times a year will get little help from the machine. Major price movements usually take several weeks or months to mature, so there is ample time to act. Day-to-day fluctuations don't really determine the market's basic trend.

The big money from tape reading is made by buying cheap and selling dear in very active markets. Yet most people are too fidgety. They never seem able to wait for a reaction on which to buy. Through an uncontrolled desire to make money by forcing things, they tend to follow the low road to failure.

▶ He Who Gets Blamed

They buy stocks near the top of a rise, anticipating higher prices. But the time inevitably comes when they are looking for higher prices only because they own stocks. This is the same thing as being a bull because you are long of stocks, rather than being long of stocks because you are a bull. When failure comes they tend to blame the broker, the Stock Exchange and, sometimes, even the company whose stock they bought, rather than themselves. Study this and mark it well: *Whatever is hard to do in the market is generally the right thing; and whatever is easy is usually the wrong thing to do.*

▶ Bull, or Bum Steer?

Before taking a position, the tape reader must decide where the situation stands with respect to the following:

1. An advance in a bull market.
2. A reaction in a bull market.

3. A decline in a bear market.
4. A recovery in a bear market.
5. A period of accumulation.
6. A period of distribution.
7. The peak of a rise.
8. The bottom of a decline.
9. A neutral, or waiting, period.

Together with price, breadth, activity, time, and volume, these factors are the principal ones that will help him form his conclusions. Past information about a company, or a stock, should interest him hardly at all. Experienced tape watchers know that once they allow any such smorgasbord of facts or gossip about corporate life to influence their way of thinking, they will lose their perspective and bury the sixth sense that all good tape traders must have.

The tape reader must be quick and pliable at all times. He must know the long and the short side of the market; he must be ready to run for cover, or hold a position without cold feet; he must be prepared to carry stocks for several days, or unload them all in five minutes. Neither pride nor prejudice can be part of his make-up. A few points' licking in a stock does not make him biased against it, for it was he who was wrong—not the tape. He has no pets, or pet hates, on the list. Industrials, rails, utilities—they are all the same to him.

▶ **"QRS"**

The stock ticker is the funnel through which flow prices that indicate the mass opinions of investors all over the world. If a man in Honolulu decides that QRS is fully valued, his action in selling the stock to a tape reader in New York, let us say, will be advertised promptly by more than 3,600 tickers operating in the United States and Canada.

Of course, the identity of the seller, or his reasons for disposing of QRS, do not concern the tape reader. He thinks only about the favorable action of the stock, which has been undergoing accumulation for several days and now seems ready for an important breakout. So he buys 200 shares at 50⅜ and immediately places a Stop Order to sell at 49, so as to limit the loss should his judgment be wrong.

QRS closes that day at 51⅛ and the next morning continues upward to 52½, where the trader unloads 100 shares. On further strength carrying to 53⅜ that afternoon, he bails out of the other 100 shares. After the market is closed, the Broad Tape (news ticker) carries the announcement of a major contract awarded the company. QRS opens the next morning at 54 on a large block, but drops back quickly under a deluge of profit taking to the 51-52 level.

The point of this example is that all during the operation, the tape reader was completely unconcerned with the background factors affecting the company and indirectly its stock. His eyes and thoughts were focused always on the tape. He cared not who sold QRS, why they did so, or what unknown factors sparked the advance. All he wanted was a short-term profit and, if QRS had gone suddenly the other way, he would have accepted the loss with no hard feelings toward the stock.

Tape reading is not an exact science, and you cannot form any simple set of rules. The results from tape trading depend solely upon the individual. The same sauce that fattens the goose might very well poison the gander. Therefore, each person must work out his own operating methods.

▶ To Each His Own

Some people trade on mechanical indications; others pin their actions on volume signals. But whatever the market climate, or the character of the background news, the tape reader should be alert at all times and ready to act.

Where the amateur fears losses and hopes for gains, the professional will have no fear. He knows when to accept a loss, just as he knows when to bag a profit. Some of his hard-earned dollars will occasionally go up the spout, but his winnings are always more numerous and are generally much larger on average.

All successful traders follow certain rules. They have proved and tested these rules by experience and they stick to them mechanically. Yet traders are also human beings, and they now and then rely on their judgment, instead of their rules. They mistakenly follow the same impulses and line of reasoning as the greenest of amateurs. Rather than thinking about what a stock is *going* to do, they think about what it *ought* to do. That is what spells the difference between "hap" and mishap.

▶ Playing Hunches

The overwhelming majority of trades made intuitively are losing trades. The same impulse that prompts a man to do such and such in the market invariably will hit thousands of other traders at the same time and perhaps for the same reason. Where the impulsive ones lose out, the deliberate, mechanical trader, whose plans are based partly on the wrong impulses of the crowd, will win. Impulsiveness and tape reading are about as amiable companions as mumps and lime juice.

The stock market is actually a tug of war. Bulls are on one team and bears on the other. The side with the greatest pulling power will show its strength on the tape and traders will be encouraged to join that side. There will be tense moments of course, when a wafer's weight could tip the balance and set the trend. The tape reader who can spot these points has much to gain and little to lose. For he can trade profitably with Stop Orders entered above or below the support and resistance levels indicated.

▶ He Who Runs May Read

A tape reader's loyalty is not pledged to any one issue. He can operate without pencil, paper, or references of any kind. His office is under his hat. He tries to anticipate market movements before they occur. He takes his cut off the loaf and passes it on. Little and often fills the purse.

The tape teaches far more than just the last sales of assorted stock issues. The activity of a stock may be noted; the quantity bought and sold indicates the extent of market interest; evidences of buying power and selling pressure will show more clearly there than elsewhere. Indeed, the tone and tendency of the market can be caught by the educated tape reader better than on the floor of the Stock Exchange.

▶ He Who Reads May Run

The ticker's story receives the closest attention of the tape reader. He respects nothing so much as the figures it prints. It records facts, not hopes or fancies. It is by the tape that the experienced trader judges supply and demand and whether stocks are being accumulated, or distributed. The novice sees only the price changes, while the well-informed tape reader sees a confirmation or contradiction of information previously received. To him it is the only guide worthy of his attention.

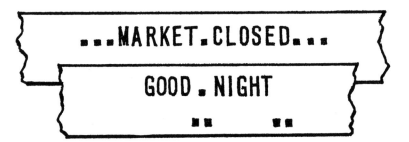

...MARKET.CLOSED...

GOOD . NIGHT

TOPICS:

- There are two forms of tape reading: (1) reading the tape to find out the prevailing market trend, or certain last sales; (2) reading the tape to weigh the trading outlook for certain stocks.
- What are some of the qualifications of a good tape reader?
- Too many statistics, opinions, reports, and résumés tend to confuse the trader and oftentimes are better left alone.
- Market movements are nearly always a surprise or a disappointment.

- The big money from tape reading is made in very active markets.
- A short story about a trade made just by following the tape.
- Mechanical indications and volume signals.
- The reasons why impulsiveness and tape reading cannot get along together.
- The ticker tape tells a continually unwinding and ever-changing story.

RULES:

1. You should be impervious to external forces and have no preconceived opinions to be a successful tape reader. Only the price changes appearing on the tape with attendant trading volume will tell you what to do and when to do it.

2. Always try to look and plan ahead, rather than considering just the last sales bobbing in front of you. The printed prices you see may have already largely discounted the news as it generally is known.

3. Tape reading is no exact science. You cannot form any definite rules, because all markets differ. Therefore, you must work out your own operational methods.

4. Be pliable at all times, but don't overtrade. Plan each campaign carefully, and never blame the tape for any error *you* may make.

5. You should be able to differentiate between what has been, what is now and what the future will be in planning a trading program.

6. Before taking a position, determine exactly where the stock you are watching, or the general market, stands. A study of price, breadth, activity, time and volume will be helpful in this respect.

7. Whatever is hard to do in the market is generally the right thing; and whatever is easy is usually the wrong thing to do.

Chapter 14

More
Turns

READING the market means: Reading "the signs of the times" all over the world; Reading about special conditions affecting domestic business and the economy; Reading the ticker tape.

Probably 99 out of every 100 traders think they can read the tape. To a certain extent they are right. But, as previously maintained, tape reading and tape interpretation are poles apart. Very likely not even one trader in a hundred picked at random would be a true tape reader.

▶ **Remember Uncle Sam**

For one thing, the greater size and breadth of the market today have compounded the difficulties of tape reading. For another, higher brokerage commissions and taxes represent two strikes against a trader even before he starts.

194

Where in former times a man could make a profit in a medium-priced issue on just a fractional rise, the stock must now advance sometimes a point or more for him to bail out even. In addition there are more people to contend with than previously.

▶ Following the Leader

In the days when stocks moved up and down in sympathy with each other, a trader could watch the tape for a blue chip issue to show its strength, and then buy another member of the same group that usually would follow the leader.

But since the market has become so selective and discriminating over the past few years, this is no longer true. To buy a stock merely because a sister stock in the group happens to be going up is folly. A man should be judged by his appearance and character, not by what his friends are like; and a stock should be judged according to the signs and signals it gives on the tape, rather than by what other stocks show. The chart will indicate *if* a move is pending and the tape will tell *when*.

▶ Accumulation and Distribution

By studying a stock's habits you will get to know it better. If it advances to a certain level and then moves rapidly up and down within a well-defined trading range, apparently unable to make much further immediate progress, it is possibly being distributed. The reverse holds true when accumulation begins after a protracted decline, and the stock seems reluctant to go much lower.

The time required for accumulation or distribution varies according to the number of shares outstanding, the state of the market and business in general, and the popularity or sponsorship of the stock itself. It may be an attractive buy while accumulation is going on, but accumulative periods are always difficult to time correctly. For this reason, it usually is wiser to postpone purchases until heavier volume carries the stock decisively through the top of its indicated trading range. The same applies to short selling when distribution is underway. The biggest profits are always made *between* the periods of accumulation and distribution.

▶ Why Don't You Do Right?

Every trader should pause now and then to seriously consider if he is doing the right thing. Following are some of the questions he should ask himself:

Am I trying to buck the prevailing trend?
Am I overtrading?
Am I following the right system?
Am I operating in the right stocks?
Am I investing, or speculating intelligently, or am I gambling?
Am I familiar with the laws of price movement?
Am I making any progress?
Am I able to afford the risks?

These are just a few of the questions you should be able to answer. Many times a person will find he has no method, is taking too many risks, does not protect himself with Stop Orders, or has failed to develop any sound judgment. To find out exactly where you stand, take an occasional mental inventory of yourself.

▶ Follow the Trend

A man who can follow a bull market up and a bear market down would seem to have all the attributes for success. Stocks always sway back and forth, so that sales on advances and purchases on dips appear to offer lucrative opportunities for the shrewd trader. However, as shown by this chart of typical bear market action, it may not always be true.

The illustration shows a series of descending tops and bottoms. In other words, each intermediate bottom reached during the declining market pictured is lower than the preceding low, while each top attained during the ensuing rally falls short of the previous top. True, profitable opportunities are available on both

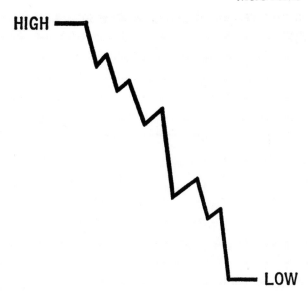

HIGH

LOW

sides of the market. But if the trader makes a mistake and buys at the wrong point, he will never "get off the hook" so long as the bear movement remains in force.

▶ Seller in the Driver's Seat

The seller, on the other hand, cannot make a mistake. To be sure, he may time a short sale incorrectly and show a temporary loss but, regardless of where he sells, provided it is not at the exact bottom, a profit lies before him. There is a tremendous advantage in determining the underlying trend accurately and following it.

A trader who believes that the market will carry lower for a year or more should not operate on the long side.* He should keep his powder dry until the normal, interim recovery phases which occur inevitably in a bear market are completed and then put out his short line. This applies also to temporary periods of reaction in a bull market when the list is honeycombed with values. A

---

* Some professionals catch the intermediate trading swings; but this is not for amateurs to try without expert guidance.

reaction in a bull market and a decline in a bear market are entirely different things.

▶ A Trader's Market

Yet there are times during an ordinary cycle when the market will be neither bullish nor bearish. This condition, known as a "trader's market," occurs usually when the market is undergoing a gradual transition from bull to bear, or vice versa, and at one or more levels during a general advance, or decline. Such periods are caused by the buying power and the selling pressure being temporarily in balance. A trader's market is something to stay away from, unless you have a good idea about the direction of the next major breakout.

Any serious student of speculation eventually learns what motivates price movements. The unwinding story of the ticker tape will tell him when definite action is about to occur. No stock will take more than a spasmodic jump, unless the basis for a sustained move has been previously prepared. When you also are prepared, then you will have valid cause for trading. But unless you are prepared, whatever you do is not investment or speculation, but gambling. You should never buy or sell against your best judgment.

▶ Negative Versus Positive

Negative events are never emphasized so much as positive ones and they are seldom long remembered. A trader will often attribute a certain market movement to some external influence that happened to coincide with it. Yet on occasion, after taking the same action as he did previously under similar circumstances, he is bewildered to find prices moving in an opposite direction. This comes from being satisfied with the obvious surface solution that was easy to interpret and happened to catch the eye.

People used to assume that hot weather was caused by comets. This was a natural deduction, since comets were seen more during the summer than at any other time of year. But comets are no more responsible for hot spells than hot spells are for them. A positive event will sit on the mind of anyone who is interested in certain effects and is looking for causes. In trying to connect events with specific causes, it is important to note two things very carefully: the occurrence of the event, and your observation of it. Many erroneous conclusions as to why stocks fluctuate are made from negligence in this respect.

▶ Is Trading a Career?

The question naturally arises if a career can be made in trading. From the standpoint of making money, trading in the stock market is *potentially* one of the most lucrative of all pursuits. There is no competition, you have no boss, no partners or employees, no overhead expenses. The working hours are good. If you want to leave stocks alone for a while, or take a vacation, the market will be at the same location, with the same opportunities, when you get back. Also, there are few restrictions as to the amount of money you need to operate.

▶ Don't Be Too Eager

But the man who makes a career of tape reading must necessarily be always striving to transact a certain amount of business at a profit. If his welfare and his family's welfare depend heavily upon the results, it follows that his operations must in some way show the degree of his eagerness to succeed.

If he is overeager, his nerves will be affected, consequently weakening his physical powers, probably damaging also his capacity to form correct judgments, and making him more liable to lose both his head and his money simultaneously in a moment of stress.

Worry or fear will sap the energy and reasoning of even the healthiest person. They won't help you a single inch along the road to success. Do not press yourself! "Speculitis" is malignant! Trade only once in a while, or whenever you are reasonably sure that the winning chances are in your favor. When too many irons are in the fire, some of them will cool.

▶ What You Need to Win

Anybody who has circulated at all among so-called financial experts and has observed them closely must know that their intelligence is above-average. They have accurate foresight, plus a capacity for judging what the general public is likely to do under certain conditions. All great traders try to gather into focus the results that are likely to stem from these circumstances. By analyzing and aligning one against the other, they are able to decide what may happen to a specific stock, or the general market, when the motivating forces are spent.

The profits made by a professional trader may be small, compared with the volume of his trades, but his losses are even smaller. He has a knack for keeping the percentages in his favor. A big trader going broke is rare indeed. Of course, there are good years and bad years, but the truth is that he does beat the fluctuations over a period of time.

However, the fact that so few speculators are *really* successful should be indication enough of the difficulties in following such a profession. Many people, after a thorough study of the field, are soon convinced that they are unsuited to the task and give it up— thanking their stars that they are cagey enough to realize the principal hazards before getting too deeply involved.

▶ Box Score

It is unfortunate that no records are kept of the number who have ventured and failed at speculation. The figures would deter many novices who are tempted or actually engaged in it. Because speculators and traders naturally keep the results of their operations secret, a newcomer to the field has no actual way of knowing how his predecessors fared, and is therefore susceptible to many of the same blunders.

Before a man begins trading he should forget about excitement. There are plenty of thrills in Wall Street, but they are likely to be expensive. Each step he takes should be deliberate; the slightest miscalculation will make him vulnerable to a loss. Continued profits are impossible without plenty of hard work. In fact the whole idea of speculation as a career, a pastime, or a business—call it what you will—involves recognition of the pursuit as a serious calling. Unless a man is willing to do so and has a special intellect, considerably above the average, he would be foolish to try and make a living in that way at all.

▶ **Speculative Triumvirate**

There are three general kinds of speculators: (1) The legitimate speculator, who devotes all or a part of his surplus capital toward buying securities which he considers to be attractive, and holding them for an expected profit. He is a leveler-up of prices and a benefit to the community; (2) The legitimate trader who sells short when individual stocks, or the market, reach levels which he believes are unusually high. He also benefits society as a leveler-down of prices; (3) The illegitimate or reckless speculator who follows the hypothesis: "Heads I win, tails you lose." His primary purpose is to win a fortune in the shortest time possible— usually starting with very little capital and no method. He ignores possible risks on the assumption that if he happens to miscalculate and show a loss, he simply can pay up and try again. None of his operations serve a useful purpose, either to the securities markets, or to himself. Under the pretense of great knowledge, he operates right and left up to the hilt. As long as fortune smiles, he will rake in the coin. But his operations are so careless, as a general rule, that he soon finds himself holding a one-way ticket on the through train to poverty.

A man with patience, perseverence and coolness, plus a business-like aptitude for laying down the elaborate machinery that is necessary for success, may make speculation his career. But if he belongs to the ordinary run of men—the haphazard speculators, who lose in the long run—he had better make plans for pursuing something much less arduous and demanding.

POINTS FOR TRADERS:

- Declines are usually broader and more rapid than advances.

- Dullness after a long decline usually foreshadows a rise.

- What grows rapidly in the market is generally short lived.

- Slow movements are usually safer to follow than fast ones.

- Beware of a stock which lags behind in an otherwise strong market.

- The market seldom remains long in one position. A violent move usually follows extreme narrowness.

- The particular merit of any stock is temporarily irrelevant when the general market is declining.

- The best trading media are stocks that are most active in terms of daily volume.

- Abnormal volume following a substantial move nearly always means that a trend reversal is imminent.

- The market always seems to be strongest at its weakest point (top) and weakest at its strongest point (bottom).

- One extreme in the market is generally followed by another in the opposite direction and with the same intensity.

- Greater activity on the decline than on the preceding advance indicates that the selling is better than the buying.

- When stocks close near their highest levels in a wide-swinging market, it is usually a bullish technical indication.

- Beware of a market that won't advance on good news. Too much good news is always a bad sign in the market.

- If a stock is unable to duplicate its highest price of a previous day, be prepared for a temporary reaction.

- If the highest level reached by the market is virtually the same for three straight days, the significance is temporarily bearish.

- The older the previous tops or bottoms are, the wider the ensuing swing will be when one or the other is penetrated.

- When the market "marks time," do likewise. It is better to look on occasionally. Rest your mind and allow your judgment to clarify.

- When an important topside resistance level is penetrated during an advance, that same level will become a support area on the next reaction.

- Stocks have a tendency to return and "fill the gap" (the space left empty on a chart) caused by a sharply higher or lower opening.

- When a stock posts a new high and then a new low, compared with its high-low of the preceding day, it is usually a sale.

- When a stock has been trending in one direction, it usually will end the movement by a sharp move followed by a quick reversal the other way.

- There is less inclination to buy at the bottom than ten points up from the bottom, and sales are more prevalent just below a top than at the exact top.

- When a relatively dormant stock fails to trade for a day or two, then becomes moderately active and finally very active, compared with its previous volume, get busy with an order pad.

- A movement may be culminating if, after a steep decline, a slow recovery gets underway, followed by another break, or after a period of market strength a slow reaction occurs followed by a vigorous rally.

- Never be discontented if you fail to sell at the top, or buy at the bottom. Extreme prices last for only a few moments. They are seldom realized by out-of-towners and not very often even by those in Wall Street.

- A market that fails to hold the ground gained during a sharp rally in the morning and closes at the bottom for the day will usually open lower the next day. The reverse is true of a declining market that rallies and closes around the day's best levels.

- When a stock supplements a previous substantial rise with another leap forward, then reacts a point or two but fails to exceed its previous high on the next swing upward, and then carries below the previous level of reaction, it is a sale. The reverse holds true in a declining market.

TOPICS:

- Reasons why proficiency in tape reading has become more difficult during the past few years.
- Today's market is ultraselective and discriminating. Stocks do not always "follow the leader," as they formerly did.
- Negative events versus positive events.
- Is trading a career? What kind of training and psychological approach are necessary for success in this field?
- A professional trader's profits may be small, compared with the volume of his trades, but his losses are even smaller. He has a knack for keeping the percentages in his favor.
- Three general classes of speculators.
- Twenty-eight points for traders.

RULES:

1. The periods *between* accumulation and distribution generally offer the most profitable opportunities.
2. Take an occasional mental inventory to find out exactly where you stand.

3. Stocks should be judged individually and on their own merits. Study their chart patterns and how they perform on the tape.

4. A reaction in a bull market and a decline in a bear market are not one and the same.

5. A "trader's market" is something to avoid, unless you have a good idea about the direction of the next important breakout.

6. Price movements are spasmodic and temporary, unless the ground work has been previously prepared for more sustained action.

7. The market never emphasizes negative events so much as positive ones. Always try to connect events with specific causes.

8. Do not press yourself! "Speculitis" is malignant!

Chapter 15

About
Watching
One's Step

HARDLY anything is more fun than making money, especially if one's own personal labor is not involved. By occasionally buying stocks when they seem undervalued and selling when they seem overvalued, many individuals have managed to gain the price of leisure to travel, pay for their children's education, or put aside a nest egg for themselves in later years. The market will never be their principal occupation, and they have no intention of ever playing recklessly with stocks. When opportunity knocks they naturally will go to the door to see what's up, yet they always follow the hypothesis that it is more important to avoid losing than to win. Losing hurts one's morale. And when they contemplate buying a stock that is expected to rise, they first of all ascertain if its earnings and dividend prospects make it reasonably loss-proof.

Most securities are bought and held on a cash basis today. For one reason, owning a stock outright is safer than holding it on margin; for another, all over-the-counter securities and most stocks selling below 5 must be paid for in full.*

▶ **No Sure Protection**

But owning stocks outright is by no means sure protection against possible loss. If you pay $10,000 for shares that decline to a value of $7,000, you obviously have a terrible paper loss that you may continue to have for several years, even though you are not compelled to sell. Many people got walloped in 1929 because they had their stocks so well-margined, or fully paid for, that they were able to hold on too long. They would have dropped less money if they had been sold out of the market on the first big dip.

We often hear of this or that stock being recommended as one "to put away in your box and forget." But no stock should ever be considered that safe. The world moves too fast today to tolerate fixed ideas, whether they be in science, art, statesmanship, business, or the stock market. The term "gilt-edged" has been tarnished by the passing years. New inventions and discoveries, changes in industry and automation are always making certain methods and products obsolete, while others are coming constantly to the fore. Before the automobile rolled into view, one-fourth of all goods sold by the biggest hardware company in the United States had something to do with a horse, a buggy, or a wagon. But how would you like to have been locked up during the early auto days with stock in a company making buggy whips? Before the Civil War canal stocks were among the most conservative of investments. And most people who owned such stocks put them

* Stocks bought on margin account for only about 25 per cent of the total shares traded on the New York Stock Exchange. Individuals in upper income brackets do two-thirds of all margin trading today.

away in their vault. But it is a strange fact that these same canal stocks reached their all-time highs shortly before they started a descent that continued all the way to zero. Investors wedded to such issues might better have held them on margin, and been obliged to sell by margin calls on the way down.

▶ What Is the Liability?

One should determine at the time of purchase just how far down a particular stock might carry—in other words, what its downside liability is—before you will believe that it is not as good as you first thought. Having decided to limit your possible loss to a predetermined amount, then you are just as safe holding the stock on margin—possibly even safer.

An old Wall Street maxim advises to "sell on the first margin call." This means that it has proved much wiser in the long run to sell enough stock to bring your account down to the broker's requirements than to put up additional margin. The fact that the broker had what he initially thought, and what you also thought, was enough margin to cover an emergency, only to find later that you were both mistaken, should be indication enough that something unfavorable has happened; and, therefore, it is no time to be meeting the call by adding more money.

▶ Here's the Pitch

The basic idea is to purchase sound, dividend-paying stocks in order to get a return on funds that might otherwise remain idle; or to strive for long-term growth, or capital gain. However, the stock market is no place for a person who lets strong convictions take root in his mind and stay there. Obstinacy may have its place among the virtues, but a mind where beliefs crystallize and won't be dislodged is not ideal for successful operations in the Street; nor is the Exchange the place for one who is temperamentally inclined to hold post-mortem examinations. Except for trying to profit by experience gained through previous transactions, you should not be always looking backward at the "might have beens." Try to forget them; otherwise, you will be perpetually unhappy. No one has ever yet made a perfect speculative trade.

▶ In on the Ground Floor

Some astute investors go to the trouble of personally visiting the plant and property of a corporation whose stock they consider buying. Anybody with a reporter's instincts and a little curiosity can keep asking questions until he is satisfied that a thing is good, or not quite so good. But there still are many people who seem unwilling to go to that much bother, or even to get more facts about a company from the research specialist of the brokerage firm with which they deal. Indeed, there is only one kind of commitment that people make with less investigation than when they buy stocks, and that is marriage. A man who would spend an hour shopping for a suit may select a stock or a wife after only the most casual study. Likewise, the same person who would seek expert advice before investing $20,000 in a home will often take a flyer on the stock of some obscure corporation. The type of man who is too lazy or bored with the idea of having to look before he leaps should entrust his money to a savings bank.

▶ Paper Profits

A sensible expenditure for something you greatly desire is one good way to realize paper profits. When you have a reasonable gain in a stock and there is something that you would really like to buy, perhaps it is a good idea to dispose of the stock and buy it. The advantage of selling a stock in which you have a profit to buy something you need, or your family needs, is not only that you make the profit permanent, but you have an opportunity to view the market from a different seat in the audience. As the saying goes: "It never hurts to put a little hay in the barn!" And suppose you take a profit to pay for a European trip and are rolling along amidst gorgeous scenery, all expenses paid by the stock market, and you note a decline in the stock you sold, how nice it is to sit back and think that you are getting something that nobody can ever take away.

Maybe you were reluctant at first to sell the stock; but, having sold, how often do you feel like buying it back immediately? It makes a tremendous difference which side of the fence you are on, and there is nothing like an unprejudiced view from the sidelines to help you to act with sanity.

▶ Wall Street Wizard

An investment trust manager had a young man in his employ who went for several weeks forecasting practically every important move up or down in about a dozen leading issues. Anyone following his predictions would certainly have made money. Yet he carried no stocks himself during that time, and that was the reason his forecasts were so good. When he finally bought for his own account, he was only moderately successful; he was then motivated by his prejudices, and was no longer free to analyze the facts in an unbiased way.

▶ Hitting the Jackpot

The most dangerous thing that can happen to a person splashing into the market and getting his feet wet for the first time is to be immediately successful. Since most of us expect something for nothing and secretly hope to get it, quick profits only help to confirm one's belief that they will come easily.

Many a man who would not expect to reach the heights as a circus clown, opera singer, or football coach, nevertheless expects to score a bull's-eye right off in the stock market. The reason for this faith in success without any special qualification is doubtless the almost universal trust in luck. But, someone says, intelligent people don't believe in luck. Ah, but they do! No matter how intelligent you may be, you have a sneaking faith in the back of your mind that some special attribute in yourself will somehow protect you from misfortune.

▶ *It Couldn't Happen to Me*

When you hear of a bad airline accident, you cannot picture yourself as being on that plane at such a time. You remind yourself: "That would never happen to me." When the insurance company forecasts that your life expectancy is a certain number of years, you secretly expect to live longer than that, because of a feeling that you are especially blessed. Everybody is like that. You see a group of fellows shooting craps. One of them has gradually lost until all his money is gone. He turns to a pal and asks, "Lend me a five-spot, will you?" He is sure that if he had just a little more money, he would win back all he lost. Likewise, a man who through a lack of the right kind of preparation or temperament has consistently been a loser in the market keeps right on trading with unfaltering faith in his eventual success. His record strongly indicates that he is not qualified for the thing he is trying to do, but he never loses faith in his ultimate good luck.

▶ *The Market Is Basically Bullish*

What makes it comparatively safe to buy and hold carefully selected stocks is the fact that the population of the world keeps growing and the demand for most goods is constantly increasing. We have become a nation of investors and speculators, mostly since our entry into World War II, but initially since the defeat of the Grand Army at Bull Run sparked Jay Cooke, "Financier of the Civil War," to hit the road with his army of well-drilled salesmen to solicit subscriptions for the Government's famous "7-30's." * Our interest in securities was furthered by the four-minute men during World War I, when they induced us to buy Liberty Bonds. Many people had never before known the satisfaction of regularly visiting a safe deposit box to clip a coupon.

---

* "Seven-Thirties" was the name derived from the fact that the bonds paid interest at 7-3/10 cents on the dollar—or $7.30 for each $100 bond. Representing two cents for every day of the year, this popular feature lifted bond sales enormously.

▶ Merits of Common Stocks

Having hit upon this improved method of saving money, we carried the idea still further and bought other bonds, not only Liberty Bonds but municipal and industrial bonds. And our financial education was just starting. Now that we had learned to buy bonds we began to think about stocks too; and not just top quality issues suitable for widows and orphans, but common stocks. The interest in common stocks was boosted greatly by a book, *Common Stocks as Long-Term Investments,* by Edgar L. Smith.

The story goes that Smith was employed by a bond house to make a far-reaching investigation and write a report proving the advantages of bonds over all other forms of securities for long-term investment. But as he delved deeper and deeper into the facts, he found that he had to prove what he hadn't intended—that the most profitable investment was a diversified list of sound, dividend-paying stocks.

▶ Wring Out the Water

The point is that we are an industrial nation and our successful industries keep growing. You buy a $1,000 bond at par and when it is due in 20 or 30 years, you get back $1,000 again. However, the $1,000 you receive is not as valuable as the $1,000 you paid in the first place: it won't buy as much. In fact, the value of the dollar has declined about 50 per cent in value during the past 25 years. Conversely, if you bought common stocks, which not only gave you a dividend claim but real ownership of part of a growing company in an expanding industry, then your stock became more valuable in proportion to the company's prosperity.

When we read in the newspapers the list of securities held by a multi-millionaire as his will is filed, we cannot help being impressed by the fact that these shrewd, rich old fellows seemed to have a great liking for common stocks. They didn't become wealthy just by squirreling their earnings away in a bank: they planted the money where it would take root, branch and grow.*

On top of the newly aroused national interest in owning securities came a long, uninterrupted period of exceptional prosperity. These earnings have been possible because the public has been drawing good wages and could buy the products that big companies have to sell. Great corporations are prosperous because we are.

▶ **Emotional Handicaps**

With stocks available today in hundreds of aggressive and well-managed, expanding enterprises, it seems as if making money in the market should be relatively easy. Indeed, profits would be much easier to realize except for the great obstacle of human nature. Here we are, the foremost industrial nation on earth, literally surrounded by companies bound to grow and become more valuable—even without taking into account the vast, untapped wonders of the space age. But what does it avail us to buy into a situation with a marvelous future if we become discouraged after a few weeks and sell our interest during a period of temporary market stalemate, or because of pessimistic gossip among our friends or the press?

▶ **The Way to Win**

Almost anybody can make up a rule for successful market operations that would be virtually sure-fire, if one were to adopt it and stick to it. The rule might be worded something like this:

Buy stocks of companies that have shown gradually increas-

---

* Money invested at 6 per cent compound interest reproduces itself in twelve years. This was well known to the Rockefellers and their advisers long ago. Frederick T. Gates, a former Baptist minister, who became the elder Rockefeller's principal adviser on business and philanthropy in the 1880's and who later headed several Rockefeller benevolent organizations, once told Mr. Rockefeller:

"Your fortune is rolling up . . . like an avalanche. You must keep up with it! If you do not it will crush you and your children and your children's children."

The 72,569 shares of Standard Oil of New Jersey with which John D. Rockefeller started the Rockefeller Foundation in 1909, were then worth $50 million. Through increased dividends, splits and market appreciation, they increased in value to $743,130,388.12 by August, 1955.

ing profits in essential industries, that is, industries making articles that people cannot well do without. But don't overtrade and don't buy until the general market indicates that it is impervious to bad news, then sell when the market has ceased to advance on good news.

Anyone who followed the basic ingredients of that simple rule would almost certainly improve his profit-making potential. But you will make your share of blunders, just as we all do, and then at the end of a period of rising prices, you may wonder how you could have failed to make more money during such a favorable time. If you are just an average person, which is altogether likely, you will probably not have the patience to make a careful enough investigation of the stocks you plan to buy; or even if you do, you may not have the fortitude to wait and try to time your intended purchases correctly.

► One Step at a Time

Some successful operators believe that the first step toward making profitable commitments in stocks should be to ascertain the tone of the general market. That should govern seven out of ten votes on the question of staying out or stepping in. The next two votes should be on the industry you intend to select, and the last vote on the particular stock. Fundamental statistics and economics are helpful, if correct—but the big danger is that they may not be correct, or that the market has already discounted them. The technical price pattern of the stock under consideration should be studied too.

Suppose that the best analysis of the situation you can make, some days after a setback has taken place, leads you to believe that we are going to have a few weeks or even months of strong recovery. Next, you study various industries and find, say, that the motion picture group will report impressive earnings during the next six months. Then, let us suppose, you find that this group of stocks has not yet discounted the favorable situation, and that price-earnings ratios, yields and so forth are more attractive than ever before. An examination of the recent technical price action of various companies in the group suggests that steady accumulation has been going on, but that the general public has not been buying to any great extent so far. It is almost inconceivable that the public would buy on a large scale in the amusement stocks quite yet, so if you see one issue in the group trying to creep higher, chances are that the impetus is being supplied by quiet insider buying.

One method of telling what the market may do is to find out how amateur traders stand and their opinion of the market. If they seem overly cautious, or better still, if they are courageously short of stocks, you can be almost certain that hundreds, perhaps thousands, are also on the sidelines, or have taken a bearish position, and you should therefore be inclined toward optimism for an advance. However, if they appear overwhelmingly bullish and are heavily loaded with stocks, you would be right in suspecting a decline.

The market he had learned, was like the sea, to be respected and feared. You sailed on its smooth surface on a placid midsummer day; you were borne along by a favoring breeze; took a pleasant swim in its waters, and basked in the rays of the sun. Or you lolled in the quiet currents and dozed. A cold gust of wind brought you to, sharply—clouds gathered, the sun had gone—there were flashes of lightning and peals of thunder; the ocean was whipped into seething waves; your fragile craft was tossed about by heavy seas that broke over its sides. Half the crew were swept overboard; you clung to a raft; the rain beat down, you drifted for days—hungry, cold. You were washed ashore. Naked and exhausted, you sank upon the beach, thankful for life itself. You looked out at the sea again; it was calm as a mill pond and sparkled invitingly, and once more the sun shone down from overhead.

Memoirs of a Trader

TOPICS:

• Some people lost money in 1929 mainly because they had their stocks so well margined, or fully paid for, that they were able to hold on too long.

• No one has ever yet made a perfect speculative operation.

• Anybody with a reporter's instincts and a little curiosity should find it profitable to visit the plant and property of a corporation whose stock he considers buying.

• A sensible expenditure for something one really needs or desires is one good way to realize paper profits.

• To be immediately successful in the market is a dangerous thing.

• Everyone believes in luck to some extent.

• Some reasons why it is comparatively safe to buy and hold carefully selected common stocks.

• Stock market profits would be much easier to realize except for the great obstacle of human nature.

• A few steps along the winning path.

RULES:

1. Owning a stock outright is safer than holding it on margin.

2. No stock is completely safe; everything contains some element of risk.

3. When buying a stock you should consider how far down it might carry in the event your judgment about it is wrong.

4. Try to avoid holding post-mortem examinations of the "might have beens" in the market.

5. There is nothing like a temporary position on the market sidelines to help clear your mind for future action.

6. Buy the stocks of companies that have shown gradually increasing earnings in industries making articles that people cannot well do without.

Chapter 16

Conclusion

FEW topics are responsible for more verbal and printed nonsense than speculation. The subject is painted sometimes for the credulous even in such a way as to border almost on deception.

Nobody has discovered the key to speculating successfully, because there is no key. No hard and fast rule can be applied with uniform success to this remarkable field; nor will any electronic computer or robot brain ever reduce it to an exact science.

The work of speculation or investment is not manual, but mental. Anything in the mind that cannot help is deadwood and should be eliminated. Belief in luck must go. Next to be cast off should be blind trust in method. Some method is necessary, of course, but only when paired with sound judgment from a mature mind. That deadly triumvirate—hope, greed and vanity—must be removed too, along with fear. Fear destroys a person's confidence and always hampers success.

You have undoubtedly met the person who complains: "When I buy a stock it goes down; when I sell it goes up." That unfortunate person has the psychology of the crowd. Because his thoughts and actions conform with the crowd, he tends to sell when he should buy and vice versa. He is a "type" whose emotional attitude typifies the mentality of the crowd; so his opinions, deeds and expressions are generally wrong relative to the market. If his opinion on the market or an individual stock is bearish, purchases may be in order. If his view of the situation is bullish, a profit may be gained by selling short. The theory is that the type is a susceptible subject for mental suggestion. He is easily influenced by what he hears and reads, or sees; and he naturally transmits what he has unconsciously absorbed.

If you tell a man something that agrees with his beliefs and opinions, or holds out the hope of profit, or tickles his vanity, he is likely to accept it—even though it may be untrue and contrary to his interests. On the other hand, if you tell him something that does not coincide with his beliefs and might cause him to lose money or suffer pain, he will listen with obvious displeasure and probably discard it, although what you said was true and contained the best advice.

Every great bull market attracts new blood, largely from the purely speculative class. Every panic introduces new investors, many of whom become speculators eventually. A few from each class make investment or speculation their regular business. This combined class has never been so large as at present.

It is depressing nonetheless to consider all the money and opportunities lost each year by the unsuspecting and the inexperienced who refuse to concede that if there was ever a spring in Wall Street from which profits could be induced to flow without plenty of hard work, it ran dry long ago.

Any study made of the developments that cause certain people to succeed where others fail would probably show that the balance between winning and losing was tipped by the individual himself every time; and that many who failed might have been successful if only they had taken the trouble to properly *train themselves.*

They tend to overlook the fact that there is no soft berth for the unskilled in the world today; nor can one hope for genuine success in the stock market or anywhere, without special education and mental training. Good intentions are worthless and industry is tossed away if the faults responsible for failure, which are largely psychological, are not controlled effectively with sufficient time and effort being devoted to really understanding the market and learning to respect and fear its capabilities.

"Something for nothing; much for little." These magic words are always received warmly in the minds of the greedy, the hopeful, the vain. If stocks are boiling up, they rush up after them; if stocks are on the downgrade, they tumble over one another to sell. Rather than trying to profit by the experience of others, they rely too much on their own ingenuity when dealing in the market place.

The hunter on safari who denies the aid of a guide and subsequently comes to grief in the jungle should expect no better epitaph than, "The penalty he paid for his stupidity was deserved." So may the average person who seeks to diminish arduous work by merely surmising future moves on the financial chessboard, anticipate a headstone no more flattering than, "He was a sucker. He dabbled in another fellow's field without understanding it."

Index